branding yourself on social media

Create a Powerful Online Presence and Build Your Personal Brand on Social Media

Content

Chapter 1

Introduction

Why Personal Branding Matters in the Digital Age

Personal branding is not a new concept, but the rise of the digital age has significantly changed the way we think about it. In the past, personal branding was mainly focused on high-profile public figures like celebrities, politicians, and CEOs. These individuals were often seen as larger than life and their personal brand was largely determined by the media and public opinion. However, with the advent of social media and the internet, personal branding has become accessible to everyone. Today, anyone can create a personal brand and use it to establish themselves as an authority or expert in their field, build their reputation, and grow their career or business.

The power of personal branding in the digital age cannot be overstated. It is no longer enough to simply have a resume or a portfolio of work. To stand out in a crowded market, you need to have a clear and compelling personal brand that sets you apart from the competition. Personal branding is all about creating a distinct identity for yourself and showcasing your unique strengths, talents, and expertise.

One of the key reasons why personal branding matters in the digital age is the sheer volume of information that is available online. With billions of people using the internet and social media, it can be difficult to get noticed or stand out. Personal branding allows you to break through the noise and establish a clear identity for yourself. By creating a cohesive and consistent brand across all your online platforms, you can make it easier for people to find and recognize you. This can be especially important for professionals who are looking to grow their business or find new job opportunities.

Another reason why personal branding is so important in the digital age is the level of transparency that exists online. With social media and review sites, it is easier than ever for people to research and learn about individuals and businesses before they decide to work with them. Personal branding allows you to take control of your online reputation and ensure that you are presenting yourself in the best possible light. By being intentional about your personal brand, you can build trust and credibility with your audience and create a positive image for yourself online.

Personal branding can also help you establish yourself as an expert or thought leader in your field. By sharing your knowledge and insights online, you can build a following of people who are interested in what you have to say. This can lead to new opportunities like speaking engagements, media interviews, and collaborations with other professionals. By becoming a go-to resource in your industry, you can build your reputation and establish yourself as a respected authority in your field.

In addition to the benefits for your career or business, personal branding can also have a positive impact on your personal life. By creating a strong and authentic personal brand, you can attract like-minded people and build meaningful relationships. This can be especially important for individuals who are looking to make a career transition or who are trying to build a network in a new city or industry.

Overall, personal branding is a crucial component of success in the digital age. It allows you to establish yourself as a distinct and recognizable entity, build trust and credibility with your audience, and grow your career or business. By creating a strong and authentic personal brand, you can differentiate yourself from the competition and stand out in a crowded market. In the following chapters, we will explore the key elements of personal branding and provide practical tips and strategies for building a powerful and effective brand online. Whether you are a business owner, entrepreneur, freelancer, or professional, personal branding can help you achieve your goals and thrive in the digital age.

Chapter 2

The Anatomy of a Personal Brand

The Anatomy of a Personal Brand: Understanding What Makes You Unique

To create a successful personal brand, it is crucial to understand what makes you unique. Your personal brand is not just a logo or a tagline; it is a reflection of your values, skills, personality, and experiences. In order to create a strong and authentic brand, you need to identify the key elements that make you stand out from the crowd.

The first step in understanding your personal brand is to identify your core values. Your values are the beliefs and principles that guide your behavior and decision-making. They are the foundation of your personal brand and should be at the center of everything you do. To identify your core values, think about the things that are most important to you. What motivates you? What do you believe in? What do you stand for? Your core values should be reflected in everything you do, from the way you communicate to the work you produce.

The next step is to identify your unique skills and talents. What are you good at? What sets you apart from others in your field? Your skills and talents should be a key component of your personal brand. They are what make you valuable to your audience and differentiate you from others in your industry. To identify your unique skills and talents, think about the things you enjoy doing and the areas where you excel. What do you do better than anyone else? What do people come to you for help with?

In addition to your values and skills, your personality is also a key component of your personal brand. Your personality is what makes you relatable and human. It is the way you express yourself and the energy you bring to your work. To identify your personality, think about the way you communicate with others. Are you outgoing and gregarious, or more introverted and reflective? Are you passionate and intense, or more relaxed and easy-going? Your personality should be reflected in your personal brand and should be consistent across all your online platforms.

Another important element of your personal brand is your experiences. Your experiences are the stories that make you who you are. They are the challenges you have overcome, the lessons you have learned, and the accomplishments you have achieved. To identify your experiences, think about the key moments in your life that have shaped you. What have you learned from your successes and failures? What have been the defining moments of your career or personal life? Your experiences should be shared in a way that is authentic and relatable to your audience.

Finally, it is important to consider your audience when building your personal brand. Your audience is the group of people you are trying to reach and influence. They are the ones who will determine the success of your personal brand. To identify your audience, think about the people you are trying to reach. What are their interests, needs, and pain points? What motivates them? What do they want to achieve? Your personal brand should be tailored to your audience and should be designed to provide value and solve their problems.

In summary, the anatomy of a personal brand is composed of your core values, unique skills and talents, personality, experiences, and audience. By understanding what makes you unique, you can create a powerful and authentic personal brand that sets you apart from the competition. Your personal brand should be a reflection of who you are and what you stand for, and should be designed to provide value to your audience. In the next chapter, we will explore how to define your personal brand and create a clear and compelling message that resonates with your audience.

Chapter 3

Defining Your Target Audience

Defining Your Target Audience: Who Are You Trying to Reach?

To build a successful personal brand, you need to know who you are trying to reach. Your target audience is the group of people who are most likely to be interested in what you have to offer. They are the ones who will ultimately determine the success of your personal brand. In order to create a message that resonates with your audience, you need to understand their needs, interests, and pain points.

The first step in defining your target audience is to identify your niche. Your niche is the area of expertise or focus that sets you apart from others in your field. It is what makes you valuable to your audience and differentiates you from your competitors. To identify your niche, think about the specific skills, experiences, or interests that you have that others in your industry may not. What are you uniquely qualified to offer? What sets you apart from others in your field? Once you have identified your niche, you can start to define your target audience.

The next step is to research your target audience. This involves gathering information about the people who are most likely to be interested in your niche. Start by identifying the demographic characteristics of your target audience, such as age, gender, education level, and income. You can also gather information about their interests, behaviors, and pain points. There are a variety of tools you can use to research your target audience, including social media analytics, surveys, and focus groups.

Once you have gathered information about your target audience, you can start to create a profile of your ideal customer. This profile, also known as a buyer persona, should describe the characteristics of the person you are trying to reach. It should include details such as their age, gender, income level, education level, and occupation. It should also describe their interests, behaviors, and pain points. The more detailed your buyer persona, the better you will be able to tailor your message to your audience.

In addition to creating a buyer persona, it is also important to consider the psychographic characteristics of your target audience. Psychographic characteristics are the attitudes, beliefs, and values that define your audience. To identify the psychographic characteristics of your target audience, think about their motivations, fears, and desires. What do they want to achieve? What are their biggest challenges? What motivates them to take action? By understanding the psychographic characteristics of your target audience, you can create a message that speaks to their needs and resonates with their values.

Finally, it is important to consider the buying cycle of your target audience. The buying cycle is the process that your audience goes through before making a purchase. It typically involves several stages, including awareness, consideration, and decision. By understanding the buying cycle of your target audience, you can create a message that speaks to their needs at each stage of the process.

In summary, defining your target audience is a crucial step in building a successful personal brand. By identifying your niche, researching your audience, creating a buyer persona, considering psychographic characteristics, and understanding the buying cycle, you can create a message that resonates with your audience and sets you apart from your competitors. Your personal brand should be designed to provide value to your audience and solve their problems. In the next chapter, we will explore how to create a clear and compelling message that communicates the value of your personal brand to your target audience.

Chapter 4

Crafting Your Brand Message

Crafting Your Brand Message: Developing a Clear and Compelling Message

Now that you have a clear understanding of your target audience, it's time to create a message that speaks to their needs and resonates with their values. Your brand message is the foundation of your personal brand. It is the message that communicates the value of your brand to your audience. A clear and compelling brand message can help you stand out from the crowd and establish yourself as an authority in your field.

The first step in crafting your brand message is to identify your unique selling proposition (USP). Your USP is the one thing that sets you apart from your competitors. It is the reason why your target audience should choose you over others in your field. To identify your USP, think about the specific skills, experiences, or interests that you have that others in your industry may not. What makes you different? What sets you apart from others in your field? Your USP should be something that is relevant to your target audience and adds value to their lives.

Once you have identified your USP, you can start to craft your brand message. Your brand message should be a concise statement that communicates your USP to your audience. It should be clear, compelling, and easy to remember. Your brand message should answer the question: "Why should I choose you over others in your field?".

To create a clear and compelling brand message, start by identifying the pain points of your target audience. What are their biggest challenges? What problems do they need to solve? Once you have identified their pain points, you can position your brand message as the solution to their problems. Your brand message should communicate the benefits of your brand in a way that resonates with your audience.

In addition to communicating the benefits of your brand, your brand message should also communicate your values. Your values are the principles that guide your actions and decisions. They are the foundation of your personal brand. By communicating your values in your brand message, you can establish yourself as a trustworthy and reliable authority in your field. Your values should be aligned with the values of your target audience.

Finally, it's important to ensure that your brand message is consistent across all of your marketing channels. This includes your website, social media profiles, email marketing, and any other channels that you use to communicate with your audience. Consistency is key to establishing a strong personal brand. Your audience should be able to recognize your brand message no matter where they encounter it.

In summary, crafting a clear and compelling brand message is an essential step in building a successful personal brand. By identifying your unique selling proposition, addressing the pain points of your target audience, communicating your values, and ensuring consistency across all marketing channels, you can create a brand message that speaks to the needs and values of your audience. Your brand message should be a concise statement that communicates the value of your brand in a way that resonates with your audience. In the next chapter, we will explore how to create a visual identity for your personal brand that reinforces your brand message and communicates your values.

Chapter 5

Creating a Brand Voice

In addition to a clear and compelling brand message, a strong personal brand also requires a unique brand voice. Your brand voice is the tone and style of your communications. It is the personality of your brand. Your brand voice should be consistent across all of your marketing channels, including your website, social media profiles, and any other channels you use to communicate with your audience.

The first step in creating your brand voice is to identify your brand personality. Think about the qualities that you want to be associated with your brand. Are you serious or humorous? Formal or informal? Energetic or calm? Your brand personality should be aligned with your brand message and your values. Once you have identified your brand personality, you can start to create your brand voice.

To create your brand voice, start by thinking about the tone and style of your communications. This includes the language that you use, the level of formality, and the overall tone of your communications. Your brand voice should be consistent with your brand personality, your brand message, and the needs of your target audience.

For example, if you have a playful and informal brand personality, you may use humor and informal language in your communications. On the other hand, if you have a serious and formal brand personality, you may use more formal language and a serious tone in your communications. The key is to be authentic and consistent in your communications.

Another important aspect of your brand voice is the use of visuals. Your visual identity should be consistent with your brand voice and reinforce your brand message. This includes the use of colors, typography, and imagery. Your visual identity should be distinctive and recognizable. It should communicate the values of your brand and appeal to your target audience.

Once you have established your brand voice, it's important to ensure that it is consistent across all of your marketing channels. This includes your website, social media profiles, email marketing, and any other channels that you use to communicate with your audience. Consistency is key to establishing a strong personal brand. Your audience should be able to recognize your brand voice no matter where they encounter it.

In addition to consistency, it's also important to listen to your audience and be responsive to their needs. Your brand voice should be adaptable to the needs of your audience. If your audience is responding positively to a particular style or tone, you may want to incorporate that into your brand voice. Similarly, if your audience is not responding well to a particular style or tone, you may want to make adjustments.

In summary, creating a unique brand voice is an essential step in building a strong personal brand. Your brand voice should be consistent with your brand personality, your brand message, and the needs of your target audience. It should be authentic, distinctive, and recognizable. Your visual identity should be consistent with your brand voice and reinforce your brand message. Finally, it's important to listen to your audience and be responsive to their needs. By establishing a strong and consistent brand voice, you can build a successful personal brand that resonates with your audience.

Chapter 6

Choosing the Right Social Media Platforms

In the world of social media, there are countless platforms to choose from. Each platform has its own unique features, audience, and style. Choosing the right social media platforms is essential to building a strong personal brand. It allows you to reach your target audience and engage with them in a way that resonates with them.

The first step in choosing the right social media platforms is to define your target audience. Who are you trying to reach? What are their demographics, interests, and behaviors? Understanding your target audience is essential to selecting the right social media channels.

Once you have defined your target audience, the next step is to research the different social media platforms. Each platform has its own unique features, audience, and style. Some platforms are better suited for visual content, while others are more text-based. Some platforms are more focused on business networking, while others are more social in nature.

Here are some of the most popular social media platforms and their key features:

- Facebook: With over 2.8 billion monthly active users, Facebook is the largest social media platform. It is a great platform for building a community and engaging with your audience through posts, groups, and live videos.

- Instagram: Instagram is a visual platform that is popular with younger audiences. It is great for showcasing visual content such as photos and videos, and for building a following through the use of hashtags and influencer marketing.

- Twitter: Twitter is a micro-blogging platform that is great for sharing short and timely messages. It is a great platform for sharing news, industry insights, and engaging in real-time conversations.

- LinkedIn: LinkedIn is a professional networking platform that is great for building your professional network and sharing industry insights. It is a great platform for B2B marketing and for building thought leadership.

- TikTok: TikTok is a short-form video platform that is popular with younger audiences. It is great for sharing fun and creative videos and building a following through the use of hashtags and influencer marketing.

- YouTube: YouTube is a video-sharing platform that is great for creating and sharing longer-form videos. It is a great platform for building an audience and generating revenue through advertising and sponsored content.

Once you have researched the different social media platforms and their key features, you can start to identify which platforms are the best fit for your personal brand. This will depend on a number of factors, including your target audience, your content strategy, and your marketing goals.

It's important to keep in mind that you don't need to be on every social media platform. It's better to focus on a few platforms that are the best fit for your personal brand and do them well. This will allow you to create a strong and consistent presence on those platforms and engage with your audience in a way that resonates with them.

In addition to choosing the right social media platforms, it's also important to optimize your profiles and content for each platform. This includes using the right visuals, captions, hashtags, and engagement tactics. Each platform has its own best practices for engagement and content creation, and it's important to follow these guidelines in order to maximize your reach and engagement.

In summary, choosing the right social media platforms is essential to building a strong personal brand. It allows you to reach your target audience and engage with them in a way that resonates with them. The key is to define your target audience, research the different social media platforms, and identify which platforms are the best fit for your personal brand. By focusing on a few platforms and optimizing your profiles and content for each platform, you can create a strong and consistent presence on social media and build a successful personal brand.

Chapter 7

Building a Strong Social Media Strategy

In order to build a successful personal brand on social media, it's important to have a strong social media strategy. A social media strategy is a plan that outlines how you will use social media to achieve your marketing and branding goals. It's a roadmap that helps you stay focused and organized, and ensures that your efforts on social media are aligned with your overall marketing objectives.

Here are some key steps to building a strong social media strategy:

1. Define your goals and objectives

The first step in building a strong social media strategy is to define your goals and objectives. What do you want to achieve through your social media efforts? Do you want to build brand awareness, generate leads, increase sales, or something else? It's important to be specific and measurable with your goals, so that you can track your progress and adjust your strategy as needed.

2. Identify your target audience

The next step is to identify your target audience. Who are you trying to reach? What are their demographics, interests, and behaviors? Understanding your target audience is essential to creating content and messaging that resonates with them.

3. Choose your social media platforms

As we discussed in the previous chapter, choosing the right social media platforms is essential to building a strong personal brand. Based on your target audience and marketing goals, choose the platforms that are the best fit for your brand and focus on those platforms.

4. Develop your brand message and voice

Your brand message and voice are the foundation of your personal brand on social media. Develop a clear and compelling message that communicates your unique value proposition and resonates with your target audience. Establish a consistent voice and tone that reflects your brand personality and values.

5. Create a content strategy

Once you have defined your brand message and voice, it's time to create a content strategy. This should include the types of content you will create, the frequency of your posts, and the themes and topics that you will cover. Your content strategy should be aligned with your marketing goals and be designed to engage and inspire your target audience.

6. Build your social media presence

With your social media strategy in place, it's time to start building your social media presence. This includes creating your profiles, optimizing your content for each platform, and engaging with your audience through likes, comments, and shares.

7. Measure and analyze your results

Finally, it's important to measure and analyze your results. Use social media analytics tools to track your performance on each platform and monitor your progress towards your marketing goals. Use this data to make adjustments to your strategy and optimize your social media presence over time.

In summary, building a strong social media strategy is essential to building a successful personal brand on social media. By defining your goals and objectives, identifying your target audience, choosing the right social media platforms, developing your brand message and voice, creating a content strategy, building your social media presence, and measuring your results, you can create a roadmap for success and ensure that your efforts on social media are aligned with your overall marketing objectives. With a strong social media strategy in place, you can build a powerful online presence, engage with your target audience, and achieve your marketing and branding goals.

Chapter 8

Developing Your Content Strategy

When it comes to building a successful personal brand on social media, developing a content strategy is key. Your content is what will attract and engage your target audience, establish your expertise, and showcase your personality and values. But how do you create content that is both engaging and valuable? Here are some tips to help you develop a content strategy that resonates with your target audience and drives results:

1. Identify your content themes and topics

The first step in developing a content strategy is to identify your content themes and topics. What are the key themes and topics that are relevant to your personal brand and of interest to your target audience? For example, if you are a fashion blogger, your content themes might include fashion trends, styling tips, and shopping guides. Make a list of the themes and topics that are most important to your brand and target audience, and use them as a basis for your content strategy.

2. Choose your content formats

Once you have identified your content themes and topics, it's time to choose your content formats. There are many different types of content formats to choose from, including blog posts, videos, podcasts, infographics, and more. Choose the formats that are the best fit for your personal brand and target audience, and that align with your content themes and topics.

3. Define your content style and tone

Your content style and tone are important elements of your personal brand on social media. They reflect your brand personality and values, and help to establish a consistent and recognizable brand voice. Define your content style and tone by considering the type of language you use, the level of formality, and the overall vibe of your content. For example, your tone might be friendly and conversational, or professional and authoritative, depending on your brand and target audience.

4. Create a content calendar

A content calendar is a schedule that outlines the topics, formats, and dates for your content. It helps you stay organized and on track with your content strategy, and ensures that you are publishing content regularly and consistently. Create a content calendar that outlines your content themes and topics, the formats you will use, and the dates you plan to publish each piece of content.

5. Research and optimize your content

In order to create engaging and valuable content, it's important to research your topics and optimize your content for search engines and social media algorithms. Use keyword research tools to identify the keywords and phrases that are most relevant to your content, and optimize your content by including those keywords in your titles, headings, and body copy. Use social media analytics tools to track the performance of your content and make adjustments as needed.

6. Engage with your audience

Finally, it's important to engage with your audience through your content. Encourage comments, likes, and shares by asking questions, providing value, and showcasing your personality and values. Respond to comments and messages in a timely and authentic way, and build relationships with your followers by showing interest in their opinions and experiences.

In summary, developing a content strategy is a key element of building a successful personal brand on social media. By identifying your content themes and topics, choosing your content formats, defining your content style and tone, creating a content calendar, researching and optimizing your content, and engaging with your audience, you can create engaging and valuable content that resonates with your target audience and drives results. With a strong content strategy in place, you can establish your expertise, showcase your personality and values, and build a loyal and engaged following on social media.

Chapter 9

Visual Branding

Visual branding is an important element of building a successful personal brand on social media. Your visual brand communicates your brand personality and values, establishes recognition and credibility, and reinforces your brand message. Here are some tips to help you develop a visual branding strategy that resonates with your target audience and drives results:

1. Define your brand aesthetics

Your brand aesthetics are the visual elements that represent your brand, such as colors, fonts, and graphic design styles. Define your brand aesthetics by considering your brand personality and values, your target audience, and your content themes and topics. Choose colors and fonts that align with your brand message and target audience, and develop a graphic design style that is consistent and recognizable across all of your social media channels.

2. Use high-quality visuals

High-quality visuals are essential for creating a strong visual brand. Use high-resolution images and videos that are clear and visually appealing, and that align with your brand aesthetics. Avoid using low-quality images or visuals that are off-brand or unappealing, as they can undermine your brand message and credibility.

3. Develop a visual content strategy

A visual content strategy is a plan that outlines the types of visuals you will use to support your brand message and engage your target audience. Choose visuals that align with your content themes and topics, and that showcase your brand personality and values. Use a variety of visuals, including photos, videos, graphics, and illustrations, to keep your content fresh and engaging.

4. Use branding elements in your visuals

Incorporating your branding elements, such as your logo and tagline, into your visuals is a great way to reinforce your brand message and increase brand recognition. Use your branding elements in your social media profile images and cover photos, as well as in your content visuals. Make sure they are prominent and clearly visible, and that they align with your brand aesthetics.

5. Be consistent

Consistency is key when it comes to visual branding. Use your brand aesthetics, visual content strategy, and branding elements consistently across all of your social media channels. This helps to establish a recognizable and consistent visual brand that reinforces your brand message and credibility.

6. Engage with your audience through visuals

Visuals are a great way to engage with your target audience and build relationships. Use visuals to showcase your personality and values, and to highlight your brand message in a creative and engaging way. Encourage your audience to engage with your visuals by asking questions, providing value, and showcasing your brand in a relatable and authentic way.

In summary, visual branding is an important element of building a successful personal brand on social media. By defining your brand aesthetics, using high-quality visuals, developing a visual content strategy, using branding elements in your visuals, being consistent, and engaging with your audience through visuals, you can create a strong visual brand that resonates with your target audience and drives results. With a strong visual brand in place, you can establish recognition and credibility, reinforce your brand message, and build a loyal and engaged following on social media.

Chapter 10

Video Marketing

Video marketing is a powerful tool for building your personal brand on social media. Video content is highly engaging, easy to consume, and allows you to showcase your personality, values, and expertise in a dynamic and creative way. Here are some tips to help you develop a video marketing strategy that resonates with your target audience and drives results:

1. Define your video goals

The first step in developing a successful video marketing strategy is to define your video goals. What do you want to achieve with your video content? Are you looking to increase brand awareness, drive engagement, or educate your audience? Once you have defined your video goals, you can create a video content strategy that aligns with them.

2. Choose the right type of video content

There are many different types of video content that you can create to support your personal brand on social media. Some examples include:

- Educational videos: These types of videos are designed to provide value to your audience by teaching them something new or sharing your expertise.

- Product or service demos: If you are selling a product or service, creating a demo video can be an effective way to showcase its features and benefits.

- Behind-the-scenes videos: These types of videos give your audience a glimpse into your life or business, and can help to build a more personal connection with your audience.

- Q&A sessions: Holding a Q&A session on video can be a great way to engage with your audience and answer their questions in a more dynamic and engaging way.

Choose the type of video content that aligns with your video goals and supports your personal brand message.

3. Use a storytelling approach

Storytelling is a powerful way to engage with your audience and communicate your brand message. Use a storytelling approach in your video content by creating a narrative that resonates with your target audience and supports your brand message. Use visuals, music, and dialogue to create a compelling and engaging story that captures your audience's attention.

4. Optimize your videos for social media

Optimizing your videos for social media is essential for ensuring that they are seen by your target audience. Use social media platforms' video features, such as captions, hashtags, and thumbnail images, to make your videos more discoverable and engaging. Keep in mind that social media platforms have different video requirements, so make sure that your videos are optimized for each platform.

5. Use professional equipment and editing software

While it's possible to create effective video content using a smartphone, using professional equipment and editing software can take your video content to the next level. Invest in a high-quality camera, microphone, and lighting equipment, and use editing software to create a polished and professional final product.

6. Engage with your audience through video

Engaging with your audience through video is a great way to build relationships and increase engagement. Use video to respond to comments, hold Q&A sessions, and showcase your personality and values. Encourage your audience to engage with your video content by asking questions, providing value, and showcasing your brand in a relatable and authentic way.

In summary, video marketing is a powerful tool for building your personal brand on social media. By defining your video goals, choosing the right type of video content, using a storytelling approach, optimizing your videos for social media, using professional equipment and editing software, and engaging with your audience through video, you can create a powerful and engaging video marketing strategy that drives results. With a successful video marketing strategy in place, you can showcase your personality, expertise, and values in a dynamic and engaging way, and build a loyal and engaged following on social media.

Chapter 11

Live Streaming

Live streaming has become an increasingly popular tool for brands to connect with their audience in real-time. Platforms like Facebook Live, Instagram Live, and YouTube Live offer an easy and effective way to interact with your audience, provide valuable content, and build your brand.

In this chapter, we'll discuss the power of live streaming and provide tips for using this tool to engage your audience and build your brand.

Why Live Streaming Matters for Your Brand

Live streaming allows you to connect with your audience in a way that pre-recorded content cannot. It provides an opportunity to interact with your audience in real-time, answer their questions, and build a relationship with them. In addition, live streaming has the ability to reach a wider audience and drive more engagement than pre-recorded content.

Live streaming is also a great way to showcase your brand's personality and values. By going live, you have the opportunity to showcase your brand's unique voice and style, and demonstrate your brand's commitment to transparency and authenticity.

Tips for Engaging Your Audience through Live Streaming

To make the most of your live streams, it's important to plan ahead and make sure you're providing valuable content that resonates with your audience. Here are some tips for engaging your audience through live streaming:

1. Plan ahead: Make sure you have a clear idea of what you want to accomplish with your live stream. Consider what topics your audience is interested in and what value you can provide to them. Plan an outline for your live stream to ensure that you cover all the important points.

2. Promote your live stream: Let your audience know about your live stream ahead of time to ensure that they tune in. Promote your live stream on your social media channels and send out reminders leading up to the event.

3. Interact with your audience: Encourage your audience to ask questions during the live stream and be sure to respond to their

comments. This will help build a relationship with your audience and increase engagement.

4. Be authentic: Live streaming is an opportunity to showcase your brand's personality and values, so don't be afraid to be yourself. Let your personality shine through and be authentic to build trust with your audience.

5. Add value: Make sure you're providing valuable content to your audience during your live stream. Share tips, advice, and insights that your audience can use to improve their lives or solve a problem.

6. Keep it short and sweet: While live streaming can be a powerful tool, it's important to keep your content short and engaging. Aim for 30-45 minutes and keep your audience engaged throughout the entire stream.

Conclusion

Live streaming is a powerful tool for building your brand and connecting with your audience. By providing valuable content and showcasing your brand's personality and values, you can build a relationship with your audience and increase engagement. With careful planning and a commitment to authenticity, you can use live streaming to take your brand to the next level.

Chapter 12

Engaging Your Audience

In the digital age, engagement is everything. It's not enough to simply post content and hope that it gets seen by your audience. To build a strong brand, you need to actively engage with your audience, build relationships, and drive engagement. In this chapter, we'll discuss the importance of engaging your audience and provide tips for building relationships and driving engagement on social media.

Why Engagement Matters for Your Brand

Engagement is an essential component of building a strong brand. It's not enough to have a large following or a lot of likes on your posts. Engagement is what drives your audience to take action, whether that's to make a purchase, sign up for your newsletter, or share your content with their own followers.

Engagement is also an important factor in the algorithms of most social media platforms. The more engagement your content receives, the more likely it is to be seen by a wider audience. This means that engagement is not just important for building relationships with your existing audience, but also for growing your audience and reaching new people.

Tips for Building Relationships and Driving Engagement

1. Respond to comments and messages: One of the simplest and most effective ways to build relationships with your audience is to respond to their comments and messages. Whether it's a thank you, a follow-up question, or a thoughtful response, taking the time to engage with your audience will go a long way in building trust and loyalty.

2. Use a conversational tone: To make your audience feel like they're having a conversation with you, use a conversational tone in your posts and replies. Use "you" and "we" to make your audience feel included, and use humor and personality to make your content more engaging.

3. Show behind-the-scenes content: Showing behind-the-scenes content is a great way to build a personal connection with your audience. Whether it's a sneak peek of your workspace, a day in the life of your team, or a glimpse into your creative process, behind-the-scenes

content can help your audience feel like they're part of your brand's journey.

4. Host giveaways and contests: Hosting giveaways and contests is a great way to drive engagement and increase brand awareness. Encourage your audience to like, comment, and share your post to enter, and offer a prize that is valuable and relevant to your audience.

5. Collaborate with other brands and influencers: Collaborating with other brands and influencers can help you reach a wider audience and build credibility. Whether it's a joint campaign, a guest post, or a co-branded event, collaborating with others can help you build relationships and drive engagement.

6. Share user-generated content: Sharing user-generated content is a great way to build relationships with your audience and showcase the value of your brand. Encourage your audience to share their own content using a branded hashtag, and share the best content on your own channels. This will help build a sense of community around your brand and encourage engagement.

Conclusion

Engaging your audience is essential for building a strong brand in the digital age. By building relationships, driving engagement, and creating valuable content, you can build trust and loyalty with your audience and drive action. With a focus on authenticity, creativity, and relationship-building, you can take your brand to the next level and create a lasting impact.

Chapter 13

The Art of Listening

Social media has become an important tool for communication, and it is not just about broadcasting your message to the world, but also listening to what others have to say. In fact, listening to your audience is an essential part of building a strong personal brand on social media. When you understand what your audience wants, you can tailor your content to their interests and build stronger relationships with them.

In this chapter, we'll explore the art of listening on social media and how you can use it to your advantage.

Understanding Your Audience

The first step in listening to your audience is understanding who they are. Your target audience should be well-defined, and you should have a clear idea of what they want and need from you. Use analytics tools to understand their demographic and psychographic characteristics, such as age, location, interests, and values.

Once you understand who your audience is, you can begin to listen to what they are saying about your brand and industry. Pay attention to the conversations and feedback they share on social media platforms. This will give you valuable insights into what they care about and how you can better serve them.

Monitoring Conversations

To listen effectively on social media, you need to monitor conversations around your brand and industry. You can use tools like social listening platforms to track mentions of your brand, product, or industry keywords.

By monitoring conversations, you can get a sense of how people perceive your brand and what they are saying about it. This will help you identify opportunities to improve your brand and build better relationships with your audience.

Responding Effectively

Once you are monitoring conversations and listening to your audience, it's important to respond effectively. Responding to feedback and engaging with your audience will show that you are listening and that you care about their opinions.

When you respond, make sure to do so in a professional and respectful manner. Even if the feedback is negative, respond with empathy and seek to understand their concerns. This will help to diffuse any negative sentiment and build trust with your audience.

Using Feedback to Improve Your Content

One of the most powerful ways to use feedback from your audience is to improve your content. When you know what your audience wants and needs, you can tailor your content to better meet their interests.

Use feedback to create content that addresses the pain points of your audience. If they have questions or concerns, create content that answers those questions and provides solutions to their problems.

Building Relationships

Listening to your audience and responding effectively can help you build stronger relationships with them. By engaging with your audience, you can create a sense of community and build a loyal following.

When you have a strong relationship with your audience, they are more likely to engage with your content, share it with their friends, and become advocates for your brand. This can help to drive more traffic to your social media profiles and increase your reach.

Conclusion

Listening to your audience is an essential part of building a strong personal brand on social media. By understanding who your audience is, monitoring conversations, responding effectively, using feedback to improve your content, and building relationships, you can create a loyal following that will help you grow your brand. Remember to always approach feedback with empathy and a willingness to learn, and use it to improve your brand and better serve your audience.

Chapter 14

Social Media Analytics

Social media has become an integral part of modern-day business and personal branding. It is essential to know how to effectively utilize the available data to measure success and improve social media strategies. In this chapter, we will delve into social media analytics, including what it is, how to collect and analyze data, and how to use the insights to improve your social media marketing strategy.

Social media analytics is the process of collecting, analyzing, and interpreting data from social media platforms to make informed decisions that can help grow your brand. The purpose of analytics is to measure the success of your social media marketing efforts and determine the areas that need improvement.

To collect data, you will need to have a business account on your chosen social media platforms, including Facebook, Twitter, LinkedIn, Instagram, and others. These platforms provide free analytics tools that allow you to view important metrics such as engagement rates, impressions, reach, and clicks.

Once you have gathered the data, the next step is to analyze it to understand what it means. This analysis will help you gain insights into your audience and their behavior. You can then use this information to make informed decisions about your content, messaging, and overall social media strategy.

Here are some of the most important metrics to track and analyze:

1. Engagement: Engagement metrics include likes, shares, comments, and other actions that users take in response to your posts. These metrics can help you understand how your audience is interacting with your brand and content.

2. Reach: Reach is the number of unique users who have seen your post. This metric is important because it can help you understand the potential audience size for your content.

3. Impressions: Impressions are the total number of times your post has been viewed, regardless of whether it was by a unique user or the same user multiple times. This metric can help you understand the overall exposure of your content.

4. Click-through rate (CTR): CTR is the number of clicks on a link in your post divided by the

number of impressions. This metric can help you understand how effective your call-to-action is.

5. Conversion rate: Conversion rate is the number of people who take a specific action, such as filling out a form or making a purchase, divided by the number of people who saw the post. This metric can help you understand the effectiveness of your social media strategy in driving specific actions.

Once you have analyzed your data and gained insights into your audience's behavior, you can use the information to improve your social media strategy. Here are some tips on how to use social media analytics to improve your strategy:

1. Identify your best-performing content: Analyze your posts to see which ones are performing the best in terms of engagement, reach, and clicks. Use this information to create more content that resonates with your audience.

2. Determine the best times to post: Look at the times and days when your audience is most active on social media. Schedule your posts for those times to increase visibility and engagement.

3. Optimize your content: Use the insights you gain from analyzing your data to optimize your content, including the format, messaging, and call-to-action.

4. Monitor and respond to comments: Engage with your audience by monitoring and responding to comments on your posts. This will help build relationships and increase engagement.

5. Continuously monitor your progress: Regularly check your analytics to track your progress and make adjustments to your strategy as needed.

In conclusion, social media analytics is a powerful tool that can help you measure the success of your social media marketing efforts and improve your overall strategy. By collecting, analyzing, and interpreting data, you can gain insights into your audience's behavior and use that information to create more effective social media content and campaigns.

Chapter 15

Hashtag Strategy

Hashtags are an essential component of social media marketing. They are a simple yet powerful way to categorize content and make it easily searchable. By using the right hashtags, you can reach new audiences, increase your visibility, and build your brand. In this chapter, we will explore the art of hashtag strategy and how to use it to build your brand on social media.

Understanding Hashtags Before we delve into the specifics of hashtag strategy, it's important to understand what hashtags are and how they work. A hashtag is a word or phrase preceded by the pound sign (#) that is used to categorize content on social media platforms. When a user clicks on a hashtag, they are taken to a feed of all the posts that have used that hashtag. Hashtags are a great way to reach new audiences who are interested in your niche or industry.

Choosing the Right Hashtags Choosing the right hashtags is crucial to the success of your social media strategy. You want to use hashtags that are relevant to your brand and the content you are posting. But you also want to use hashtags that are popular enough to attract a large audience. Using too niche or obscure hashtags can limit your reach, while using overly popular hashtags can cause your content to get lost in the sea of other posts.

One strategy for choosing the right hashtags is to research popular hashtags within your niche or industry. You can use tools like Hashtagify or RiteTag to find popular hashtags related to your brand. You can also look at the hashtags your competitors are using and incorporate them into your own strategy.

Another strategy is to create your own branded hashtags. Branded hashtags are unique to your brand and can help increase brand awareness and create a community around your brand. Make sure to choose a branded hashtag that is easy to remember and relevant to your brand.

Using Hashtags Effectively Once you have chosen your hashtags, it's important to use them effectively. Here are some tips for using hashtags on social media:

1. Don't overuse hashtags: Using too many hashtags can make your posts look spammy and reduce engagement. Stick to 2-5 hashtags per post.

2. Use location-based hashtags: If you are a local business, using location-based hashtags can help you reach a local audience.

3. Use trending hashtags: Using trending hashtags can help increase your visibility and attract new followers.

4. Use branded hashtags consistently: Consistently using your branded hashtags can help increase brand awareness and build a community around your brand.

5. Mix up your hashtags: Don't use the same hashtags in every post. Mix up your hashtags to attract new audiences and keep your content fresh.

Measuring Hashtag Success Measuring the success of your hashtag strategy is crucial to improving your social media strategy. Social media analytics can help you track which hashtags are driving the most engagement and which ones are falling flat. You can use tools like Sprout Social or Hootsuite to track the success of your hashtags.

When measuring the success of your hashtags, it's important to look at engagement metrics like likes, comments, and shares. You can also track the reach and impressions of your hashtags to see how many people your content is reaching.

Conclusion Hashtag strategy is a powerful tool for building your brand and reaching new audiences on social media. By choosing the right hashtags and using them effectively, you can increase your visibility, drive engagement, and build a community around your brand. Remember to measure the success of your hashtag strategy and make adjustments as needed to improve your social media strategy.

Chapter 16

Influencer Marketing

In today's digital age, it's becoming increasingly important for brands to engage with their target audiences in an authentic and meaningful way. One of the most effective ways to do this is through influencer marketing. In this chapter, we'll explore the power of influencers and how you can leverage their influence to build your brand.

Influencer marketing is a type of social media marketing where brands partner with influencers, people who have a large following on social media, to promote their products or services. The influencer promotes the brand to their followers, typically through sponsored posts or endorsements, and in turn, the brand benefits from the influencer's credibility and reach.

The rise of influencer marketing can be attributed to the shift in consumer behavior. As consumers become increasingly skeptical of traditional advertising, they turn to influencers for recommendations and product reviews. In fact, a recent survey found that 82% of consumers are likely to follow a recommendation made by an influencer.

When it comes to choosing the right influencer, there are a few things to consider. First, you'll want to look for influencers who align with your brand values and target audience. For example, if you're a beauty brand targeting millennials, you may want to partner with a popular beauty influencer who has a large following of millennial women.

Another factor to consider is the influencer's engagement rate. An influencer may have a large following, but if their engagement rate is low, it may not be worth partnering with them. Look for influencers who have a high engagement rate, meaning their followers are actively engaging with their content.

Once you've identified the right influencer, it's important to establish a clear partnership agreement. This should outline the scope of the partnership, the deliverables, and any compensation. It's also important to ensure that the partnership is disclosed properly, so that your audience knows that the influencer is promoting your product or service.

When it comes to the content that the influencer will create, it's important to strike a balance between promoting your brand and maintaining the influencer's authentic voice. The best influencer partnerships are those that feel natural and genuine.

So, instead of dictating exactly what the influencer should say, give them the freedom to create content that feels true to their brand and style.

Finally, it's important to measure the success of your influencer marketing campaign. Look at metrics like engagement, reach, and conversion rates to determine if the campaign was effective. And don't be afraid to make changes and pivot your strategy if necessary.

In conclusion, influencer marketing can be a powerful tool for building your brand in the digital age. By partnering with the right influencers and creating authentic content that resonates with your target audience, you can reach new audiences and build strong relationships with your customers. Just remember to approach influencer marketing with a clear strategy, and always prioritize authenticity and transparency.

Chapter 17

Networking on Social Media

Social media has completely changed the way we communicate and connect with others. It has transformed the way we network and build professional relationships. In the past, networking often involved attending industry events and conferences, handing out business cards, and scheduling face-to-face meetings. While those tactics are still valuable, social media has made networking easier, more accessible, and more efficient than ever before.

In this chapter, we'll discuss how to effectively network on social media, build relationships with others in your industry, and use those connections to grow your personal brand and business.

1. Why Networking on Social Media Matters The power of networking has always been a driving force in business. Connecting with others in your industry can lead to new opportunities, collaborations, and even friendships. But in the digital age, networking has taken on a whole new meaning. By using social media to network, you have access to a global community of

professionals at your fingertips. This can help you expand your reach and open doors that you may not have been able to access before.

2. Identifying and Finding Your Network The first step to networking on social media is identifying and finding the right people to connect with. Start by making a list of individuals or companies that you admire, are in your industry, or share similar interests. Use social media platforms such as LinkedIn, Twitter, and Facebook to search for these people or companies. You can also join online groups or communities related to your industry to connect with like-minded individuals.

3. Engaging with Your Network Once you have identified your network, the next step is to engage with them. Start by following their accounts, liking their posts, and sharing their content. Engage with them by leaving thoughtful comments on their posts or sharing your own insights on industry-related topics. Be genuine in your interactions and remember that networking is all about building meaningful relationships.

4. Collaborating and Building Relationships Networking on social media can lead to more

than just online conversations. It can also lead to real-life collaborations and partnerships. When you engage with individuals in your network, keep an eye out for opportunities to collaborate. Look for ways that you can work together on projects, share resources, or even refer clients to one another. Building these types of relationships can be beneficial to both parties and can help you grow your business or personal brand.

5. Being Authentic and Professional While social media is a more informal and relaxed environment, it's important to maintain a professional demeanor when networking. Avoid oversharing or posting inappropriate content, as this can harm your personal brand and reputation. Always be authentic in your interactions, but also be mindful of your tone and the impression that you are making on others.

6. Staying Organized Networking on social media can quickly become overwhelming if you don't stay organized. Use tools such as social media management software or a spreadsheet to keep track of your contacts, conversations, and collaborations. This will help you stay on top of

your networking efforts and ensure that you are following up with important contacts.

7. Continuously Building Your Network
Networking on social media is an ongoing process. You should always be looking for new ways to expand your network and connect with others in your industry. Make it a habit to regularly search for and follow new accounts, engage with your existing network, and participate in industry-related discussions and events.

In conclusion, networking on social media is an essential component of building a strong personal brand and growing your business. By identifying and engaging with the right people, collaborating and building relationships, and staying organized, you can effectively network and establish a strong presence in your industry. Remember to always be authentic, professional, and continuously build your network to stay ahead of the curve.

Chapter 18

Collaborations

In the world of social media, collaborations can be a powerful way to build relationships and promote your brand. By working with other businesses, influencers, and content creators, you can expand your reach, build your reputation, and create engaging content that resonates with your audience.

But how do you go about finding collaborators and creating successful partnerships? In this chapter, we'll explore the art of collaborations and provide you with practical tips and strategies for building relationships and cross-promoting your brand.

Why Collaborate?

There are many benefits to collaborations on social media. Here are just a few reasons why you might want to consider collaborating with others:

1. Expand your reach: By partnering with other businesses or influencers, you can tap into their existing audience and reach new people who might not have discovered your brand otherwise.

2. Create engaging content: Collaborations often result in creative, dynamic content that resonates with your audience and keeps them engaged.

3. Build relationships: Collaborations can help you build meaningful relationships with other businesses or individuals in your industry, which can lead to future opportunities and partnerships.

4. Cross-promote: Collaborating allows you to promote your brand to a new audience while also promoting your collaborator to your existing audience, creating a win-win situation.

Finding the Right Collaborator

The first step in any successful collaboration is finding the right partner. You want to find someone who shares your values, target audience, and goals. Here are a few tips for finding the right collaborator:

1. Identify your goals: Before you start looking for a collaborator, you need to have a clear idea of what you want to achieve from the partnership. Do you want to reach a new audience? Create engaging content? Build relationships?

Knowing your goals will help you identify the right collaborator.

2. Research potential partners: Look for businesses or influencers in your industry who share your values and target audience. Check out their social media channels and see if their content aligns with your brand.

3. Reach out: Once you've identified a potential collaborator, reach out to them with a personalized message. Let them know why you think a collaboration would be beneficial and how it aligns with your goals.

Creating a Successful Partnership

Once you've found the right collaborator, it's time to start creating content together. Here are a few tips for creating a successful partnership:

1. Set clear goals: Make sure you and your collaborator are on the same page about what you want to achieve from the collaboration. This will help ensure that you're both working towards the same goals.

2. Define roles: Clearly define each person's role in the collaboration. Who will create the content? Who will be responsible for promoting it?

Having clear roles will help ensure that everyone is on the same page.

3. Be creative: Collaborations offer a unique opportunity to create engaging, creative content that resonates with your audience. Brainstorm ideas with your collaborator and think outside the box.

4. Communicate regularly: Keep in touch with your collaborator throughout the process to ensure that everything is going smoothly. Regular communication will help you address any issues or concerns that arise.

5. Cross-promote: Make sure you're both promoting the collaboration to your respective audiences. This will help you reach a new audience while also promoting your collaborator to your existing audience.

Measuring Success

As with any social media strategy, it's important to measure the success of your collaboration. Here are a few metrics you might want to track:

1. Reach: How many people saw the content?

2. Engagement: How many people liked, commented on, or shared the content?

3. Follower growth: Did you gain new followers as a result of the collaboration?

4. Sales: Did the collaboration lead to an increase in sales?

When it comes to collaborations, there are several different ways you can approach them. Here are a few strategies to consider:

1. Co-Branding: Co-branding is when two or more brands come together to create a product or service. This can be a great way to combine your strengths and create something unique that appeals to both of your audiences. For example, Nike and Apple teamed up to create the Nike+ app, which tracks your runs and syncs with your music.

2. Influencer Collaborations: Working with influencers can be an effective way to reach new audiences and build credibility. You can collaborate with influencers in several different ways, such as creating sponsored content or partnering on a product launch. The key is to find influencers who align with your brand

values and have a following that overlaps with your target audience.

3. Guest Blogging: Guest blogging is when you write a blog post for another website or invite someone to write a post for your site. This can be a great way to cross-promote your brand and reach new audiences. When guest blogging, it's important to choose sites that align with your brand values and have a similar audience.

4. Social Media Takeovers: A social media takeover is when you give someone else control of your social media accounts for a day or week. This can be a great way to inject some new energy into your social media presence and reach new audiences. Just make sure to choose someone who aligns with your brand values and has a following that overlaps with your target audience.

5. Cross-Promotions: Cross-promotions are when two brands promote each other's products or services. This can be a great way to reach new audiences and leverage the strengths of both brands. For example, a fashion brand might team up with a beauty brand to offer a bundle deal.

When it comes to collaborations, the key is to find partners who align with your brand values and have a similar audience. You want to create something that feels authentic and provides value to both of your audiences.

Another important factor to consider is the logistics of the collaboration. Make sure to set clear expectations upfront, including deadlines, deliverables, and compensation. This will help ensure that both parties are on the same page and that the collaboration runs smoothly.

Overall, collaborations can be a powerful tool for building your brand and reaching new audiences. Whether you're working with another brand or an influencer, the key is to find partners who align with your values and can help you achieve your goals.

Chapter 19

Building Your Email List

In today's digital age, many marketers have been drawn to the flashy and constantly-evolving world of social media. However, while social media is undoubtedly a powerful tool for building brand awareness and engaging with audiences, there is another tool that should not be overlooked: email marketing.

Email marketing is a powerful tool for building relationships with your audience, keeping them engaged, and driving conversions. In fact, studies have shown that email marketing can have a return on investment (ROI) of up to 4400%. This means that for every $1 spent on email marketing, you can expect an average return of $44.

But in order to reap the benefits of email marketing, you first need to build a strong email list. In this chapter, we will discuss the importance of building an email list, and provide you with some tips on how to do so effectively.

Why Building an Email List Matters

An email list is a collection of email addresses that you have gathered from people who are interested in your brand or content. These email addresses can be used to send out newsletters, promotional messages, updates, and other information that is relevant to your audience.

Building an email list is important for a number of reasons:

1. Direct communication with your audience: Unlike social media, email provides a direct line of communication with your audience. When you send an email, it goes directly to your subscribers' inboxes, where they are more likely to see it and engage with it.

2. Increased engagement: People who sign up for your email list are usually more engaged with your brand than those who follow you on social media. By providing them with valuable content and building a relationship with them through email, you can increase their engagement even further.

3. Higher conversion rates: Because email marketing is a more personal and targeted form of marketing, it often has higher conversion rates than other forms of marketing.

By building a strong email list, you can increase the chances of converting subscribers into customers.

4. Greater control: With social media algorithms constantly changing, it can be difficult to ensure that your content is seen by your audience. By building an email list, you have greater control over who sees your content and when.

How to Build Your Email List

Now that we have discussed the importance of building an email list, let's take a look at some strategies for doing so effectively:

1. Create valuable lead magnets: A lead magnet is a piece of content that you offer to your audience in exchange for their email address. This can be an e-book, a whitepaper, a webinar, or anything else that provides value to your audience.

2. Optimize your website: Make sure that your website is optimized for collecting email addresses. This can include placing opt-in forms in strategic locations, such as your homepage, your blog, and your landing pages.

3. Run contests and giveaways: Contests and giveaways can be a great way to incentivize people to sign up for your email list. Make sure that the prize is relevant to your audience and provides value.

4. Use social media to promote your email list: Use your social media channels to promote your email list and encourage people to sign up. You can do this by creating social media posts that promote your lead magnets or highlight the benefits of joining your email list.

5. Attend events and collect email addresses: If you attend conferences or events, make sure that you have a way to collect email addresses. This can be as simple as bringing a clipboard and sign-up sheet, or using a lead capture app on your phone.

Social media is undoubtedly a powerful tool for building your personal brand, but it's important not to forget about the power of email marketing. Email marketing has been around for a long time, and while it may not be as glamorous as some of the newer social media platforms, it remains one of the most effective ways to reach your audience.

The reason email marketing is so effective is that it allows you to communicate with your audience in a more personal and direct way. When someone gives you their email address, they are giving you permission to communicate with them, which is a powerful thing. With social media, your message is competing with a lot of other noise, but with email, you have a much better chance of getting your message in front of your audience.

So how do you go about building your email list? Here are some tips to get you started:

1. Offer something of value

The best way to get people to give you their email address is to offer them something of value in return. This could be a free guide, an e-book, or a discount code. Whatever it is, make sure it's something that your target audience will find valuable and relevant.

2. Use opt-in forms

Opt-in forms are a great way to collect email addresses. These are forms that you place on your website or social media profiles that allow people to sign up for your email list. Make sure your opt-in forms are clear and easy to use, and that you provide a clear explanation of what people can expect to receive when they sign up.

3. Use social media to promote your email list

Social media is a great way to promote your email list and encourage people to sign up. Make sure you have a clear call-to-action in your social media posts and that you provide a link to your opt-in form.

4. Use your existing email list

If you already have an email list, use it to your advantage. Encourage your existing subscribers to share your emails with their friends and family, and provide incentives for them to do so.

Once you have built your email list, it's important to use it effectively. Here are some tips for using email marketing to strengthen your brand:

1. Provide value

Just like with your social media content, it's important to provide value with your emails. Make sure you are sending emails that are relevant and useful to your audience.

2. Personalize your emails

Personalization is key when it comes to email marketing. Use your subscriber's name in the subject line and opening sentence of your email, and make sure the content is tailored to their interests.

3. Segment your list

Segmenting your email list allows you to send targeted emails to specific groups of people. This can be based on demographics, interests, or any other criteria that you choose.

4. Test and optimize

As with any marketing strategy, it's important to test and optimize your email campaigns. Use A/B testing to try out different subject lines and content, and use analytics to measure the success of your campaigns.

In conclusion, email marketing may not be as trendy as some of the newer social media platforms, but it remains one of the most effective ways to build and strengthen your personal brand. By following these tips, you can build a strong email list and use email marketing to communicate with your audience in a more personal and direct way.

Chapter 20

Podcasting

In recent years, podcasting has become a popular medium for building a personal brand and establishing thought leadership. It offers a unique way for creators to connect with their audience and share their expertise through audio content. In this chapter, we'll explore how you can leverage podcasting to build your brand and expand your reach.

Why Podcasting?

Podcasting is a powerful medium that offers several advantages for building your brand. First, it allows you to create audio content that is engaging, informative, and easy to consume. Unlike video content, which requires your audience to watch and listen, podcasting allows your listeners to multitask while consuming your content. They can listen while they're commuting, working out, or doing other tasks.

Second, podcasting offers a way to establish thought leadership in your industry. By creating high-quality, informative content, you can demonstrate your expertise and build credibility with your audience.

This can help you stand out in a crowded market and attract new clients, customers, or followers.

Finally, podcasting offers a way to build a loyal audience. Because podcast listeners often form a connection with the host, they are more likely to become loyal fans and advocates for your brand. This can lead to increased engagement, more social shares, and higher conversions.

Getting Started with Podcasting

Before you start podcasting, it's important to have a clear understanding of your goals and target audience. Consider the following questions:

- What topics do you want to cover in your podcast?

- Who is your target audience, and what kind of content are they interested in?

- How often do you want to publish new episodes?

- What is your overall objective for your podcast?

Once you have a clear idea of your goals and audience, you can start planning your podcast. Here are some steps to get started:

1. Choose your format: There are several podcast formats to choose from, including solo shows, interview-style shows, panel discussions, and more. Choose a format that works best for your audience and goals.

2. Develop your content strategy: Determine what topics you want to cover in your podcast and create a content calendar to plan out your episodes. Consider what your audience wants to learn, and how you can add value with your content.

3. Choose your equipment: To start a podcast, you'll need a microphone, headphones, and recording software. There are several options to choose from, ranging from basic setups to professional-grade equipment.

4. Record and edit your episodes: Once you have your equipment set up, it's time to start recording your episodes. Make sure you have a quiet environment to record in, and practice speaking clearly and confidently. Once you've recorded your episode, edit it for length and clarity.

5. Publish and promote your episodes: Once your episode is complete, it's time to publish and

promote it. Upload your episode to a podcast hosting platform like Buzzsprout or Libsyn, and promote it on social media, your website, and other relevant channels.

Tips for Successful Podcasting

Here are some tips to help you create a successful podcast:

1. Be consistent: Consistency is key when it comes to podcasting. Choose a regular publishing schedule and stick to it. This will help your audience know when to expect new episodes and keep them engaged.

2. Be authentic: Authenticity is important in podcasting. Don't be afraid to share your personality and opinions in your episodes. This will help you connect with your audience and build a loyal following.

3. Be engaging: Make sure your episodes are engaging and interesting to listen to. Use storytelling and humor to keep your audience interested.

4. Promote your podcast: Don't be afraid to promote your podcast on social media and

other relevant channels. This will help you attract new listeners and build your brand.

Benefits of Social Media Advertising

Social media advertising offers several key benefits for businesses looking to promote their brand. First and foremost, it allows you to reach a highly targeted audience. Social media platforms such as Facebook and Instagram allow you to target users based on factors such as age, gender, location, interests, and more. This means that your ads will be seen by the people most likely to be interested in your product or service.

In addition, social media advertising can be cost-effective. While traditional forms of advertising such as TV commercials and billboards can be expensive, social media advertising can be done on a smaller budget. You can set a daily or weekly ad spend limit and only pay for the clicks or impressions your ads receive.

Types of Social Media Ads

There are several types of social media ads you can use to promote your brand. Here are a few examples:

1. Sponsored Posts - Sponsored posts are promoted posts that appear in a user's social

media feed. They can be used to promote a product or service, or to share a piece of content such as a blog post or video.

2. Display Ads - Display ads are visual ads that appear on the side or bottom of a user's social media feed. They can be static images or animated graphics.

3. Video Ads - Video ads are short promotional videos that appear in a user's social media feed. They can be used to promote a product or service, or to tell a brand's story.

4. Carousel Ads - Carousel ads are a series of images or videos that users can swipe through to see multiple products or services.

Creating a Successful Social Media Advertising Campaign

To create a successful social media advertising campaign, it's important to understand your target audience and their interests. You can use the targeting options available on social media platforms to reach the people most likely to be interested in your product or service.

It's also important to create compelling ad content that will capture the attention of your audience. This can be achieved through eye-catching visuals, a clear message, and a strong call-to-action.

In addition, it's important to track the performance of your ads and make adjustments as needed. Social media advertising platforms offer analytics and reporting tools that can help you measure the success of your campaigns and make changes to improve their performance.

Conclusion

Social media advertising can be a highly effective way to promote your brand and reach a targeted audience. By understanding the benefits of social media advertising, the various types of social media ads, and how to create a successful advertising campaign, you can use this powerful tool to grow your brand and increase your online visibility.

Chapter 21

Writing a Book

In the world of personal branding, writing a book can be a powerful way to establish your authority and expertise. A book can be seen as a tangible manifestation of your knowledge and experience, and can serve as a valuable tool for building your brand and expanding your reach.

Writing a book can seem like a daunting task, but with the right mindset and approach, it can be a rewarding experience that not only establishes your expertise, but also helps you to clarify your own thoughts and ideas.

In this chapter, we'll explore why writing a book is such an effective tool for building your personal brand, and we'll provide some tips and strategies for getting started on your own book-writing journey.

Why Writing a Book Matters

There are many reasons why writing a book can be a valuable tool for building your personal brand. Here are a few of the most important:

1. Establishes your authority and expertise: When you write a book on a topic, you are essentially declaring yourself an expert in that field. This can help to establish your authority and credibility with your target audience, and can help to differentiate you from others in your industry.

2. Builds trust with your audience: A book is a tangible representation of your ideas and expertise, and can help to build trust with your audience. When someone reads your book, they are essentially inviting you into their world and trusting you to provide value and insight.

3. Provides a platform for your ideas: A book is a powerful platform for sharing your ideas with the world. It allows you to delve deeply into a topic and to present your ideas in a clear, structured way.

4. Expands your reach: A book can help to expand your reach and bring your ideas to a wider audience. It can serve as a powerful marketing tool for your brand, and can help to attract new followers and customers.

Getting Started

If you're interested in writing a book, the first step is to get clear on your topic and your goals. Here are some questions to consider:

1. What is the main topic of your book? What do you want to communicate to your readers?

2. Who is your target audience? Who do you want to reach with your book?

3. What are your goals for the book? Do you want to establish yourself as an expert in your field? Do you want to build your brand and expand your reach? Do you want to drive sales of your products or services?

Once you have a clear idea of your topic and goals, it's time to start outlining your book. Here are some tips for getting started:

1. Start with a clear structure: Begin by outlining the main sections and chapters of your book. This will help you to organize your ideas and ensure that your book has a clear and logical flow.

2. Identify your key messages: Think about the key messages that you want to communicate in your book, and make sure that these are reflected in your chapter outlines.

3. Break it down: Writing a book can seem overwhelming, so break the process down into smaller, more manageable steps. For example, set a goal of writing a certain number of words each day, or aim to complete a certain number of chapters each week.

4. Stay focused: Writing a book can be a time-consuming process, so it's important to stay focused and motivated. Set aside time each day or week to work on your book, and try to eliminate distractions and interruptions.

Writing a book can be an incredibly effective way to establish your authority and expertise in your industry, and to build your personal brand. Whether you're a business owner, entrepreneur, or expert in your field, a book can be a powerful tool for building your brand and sharing your message with the world.

One of the key benefits of writing a book is that it allows you to establish yourself as an expert in your field. By sharing your knowledge and insights with your audience, you can position yourself as a thought leader and gain credibility in your industry. This can open up new opportunities for speaking engagements, media appearances, and partnerships, all of which can further enhance your brand and help you reach new audiences.

In addition to establishing your authority, writing a book can also help you to build your brand by creating a deeper connection with your audience. A book allows you to share your personal story, your values, and your unique perspective on your industry. This can help your readers to feel a deeper connection with you, and to develop a sense of loyalty to your brand.

Of course, writing a book is a significant undertaking, and it's not something to be taken lightly. It requires a significant investment of time and effort, and it can be a challenging and sometimes frustrating process. However, the rewards can be substantial, and if you're committed to your brand and your message, then writing a book can be one of the most powerful ways to build your personal brand and grow your business.

In order to get started with writing a book, it's important to first identify your topic and your target audience. What is the message you want to share with the world, and who do you want to reach with that message? Once you have a clear idea of your topic and your audience, you can begin to develop an outline and start writing.

It's important to remember that writing a book is a marathon, not a sprint. It's likely to take several months or even years to complete your book, and there will be times when you feel frustrated or discouraged. However, by staying focused on your goal and maintaining a consistent writing routine, you can make steady progress and ultimately achieve your goal of publishing a book.

One of the keys to successful book writing is to be organized and disciplined in your approach. Set aside specific times each week to write, and establish a clear plan for how you will structure and organize your book. Whether you're writing a memoir, a how-to guide, or a business book, it's important to have a clear vision for what you want to achieve and how you want to convey your message to your audience.

Another important aspect of writing a book is to be authentic and true to your brand. Your readers will be looking to you as a trusted source of information and advice, so it's important to be genuine and honest in your writing. Be sure to stay true to your values and your unique perspective on your industry, and be willing to share your personal story and experiences with your audience.

In conclusion, writing a book can be a powerful way to build your personal brand and establish your authority in your industry. By sharing your knowledge and insights with your audience, you can position yourself as a thought leader and gain credibility in your field. Although it can be a challenging and time-consuming process, the rewards can be substantial, and if you're committed to your brand and your message, then writing a book can be one of the most effective ways to build your personal brand and grow your business.

Chapter 22

Guest Blogging

As a personal brand, it's important to establish yourself as an expert in your industry. One way to do this is by writing for other websites through guest blogging. Guest blogging can be a powerful tool for building your brand, expanding your reach, and establishing your authority in your field. In this chapter, we'll discuss how guest blogging can benefit your personal brand and provide tips for creating effective guest blog posts.

The Benefits of Guest Blogging

Guest blogging offers a variety of benefits for personal brands. Here are a few of the main advantages:

1. Increased exposure: When you write for another website, you have the opportunity to reach a new audience that may not be familiar with your brand. This can help you expand your reach and attract new followers.

2. Establish authority: By sharing your knowledge and expertise on a particular topic, you can establish yourself as an authority in your field.

This can help you build trust with your audience and establish your brand as a go-to resource in your industry.

3. Building backlinks: Many websites will allow you to include a link to your own website in your guest post. This can help you build backlinks to your site, which can improve your search engine rankings and drive more traffic to your site.

Tips for Creating Effective Guest Blog Posts

To get the most out of your guest blogging efforts, it's important to create high-quality, engaging content that provides value to the website's audience. Here are a few tips to help you create effective guest blog posts:

1. Choose the right website: When selecting a website to write for, it's important to choose a site that is relevant to your industry and has an audience that aligns with your target audience.

2. Research the website's content: Before writing your guest post, take some time to read through the website's existing content. This will give you a better understanding of the types of

topics and writing styles that resonate with their audience.

3. Focus on providing value: Your guest post should provide value to the website's audience. Make sure your post is informative, engaging, and provides actionable takeaways for the reader.

4. Write in the website's tone and style: To ensure your post fits seamlessly with the website's existing content, it's important to write in the website's tone and style. This will help your post resonate with their audience and establish a connection with them.

5. Include a call to action: At the end of your post, include a call to action that directs readers to your website or social media profiles. This can help you build your audience and expand your reach.

In conclusion, guest blogging can be a valuable tool for personal brands looking to expand their reach, establish their authority, and build their audience. By following these tips and providing high-quality content that provides value to the website's audience, you can create effective guest blog posts that benefit both you and the website you're writing for.

Chapter 23

Creating Your Own Blog

Blogging is an excellent way to establish your brand and establish yourself as an authority in your field. With the rise of the internet, blogs have become increasingly popular, and they offer an ideal platform for building your brand and creating a loyal following. In this chapter, we'll explore the benefits of blogging and offer tips on how to create and maintain a successful blog.

Why Blogging Matters

Blogging is a powerful tool for building your brand and online presence. By creating quality content that is relevant and valuable to your audience, you can establish yourself as an authority in your field. Blogging also allows you to build a community of loyal followers who engage with your content and share it with others, further expanding your reach.

In addition, blogging is an excellent way to drive traffic to your website and social media channels. By incorporating relevant keywords and topics into your blog posts, you can increase your visibility in search engine results and attract new visitors to your website.

Creating a Successful Blog

Creating a successful blog takes time and effort, but the rewards are worth it. Here are some tips to help you create and maintain a successful blog:

1. Define Your Audience: Before you start writing, it's essential to identify your target audience. Who are you writing for, and what topics are they interested in? By understanding your audience, you can create content that is relevant and valuable to them.

2. Choose Your Niche: With so many blogs online, it's crucial to differentiate yourself by choosing a specific niche or topic. Choose a topic that you are passionate about and have expertise in, and that is not too broad.

3. Develop a Content Strategy: Creating quality content consistently is essential for building a successful blog. Develop a content strategy that includes the topics you will cover, the frequency of your posts, and your promotion plan.

4. Write Engaging Content: Your content should be engaging, informative, and easy to read. Use

a conversational tone, and keep your posts focused and organized.

5. Incorporate Visuals: Adding visuals such as images, infographics, and videos can make your blog posts more engaging and shareable.

6. Promote Your Blog: Promoting your blog is crucial to building your audience. Share your blog posts on your social media channels and participate in online communities related to your niche.

7. Engage with Your Audience: Building relationships with your readers is essential for growing your blog. Respond to comments and encourage engagement with your content.

Conclusion

Creating a successful blog takes time, effort, and dedication, but the benefits are worth it. By creating quality content that is relevant and valuable to your audience, you can establish yourself as an authority in your field and build a loyal following. Use the tips outlined in this chapter to create and maintain a successful blog that helps you build your brand and establish yourself as an authority online.

Chapter 24

Social Media Advertising

As social media platforms continue to evolve, paid advertising has become an increasingly important tool for building your brand and reaching new audiences. With the ability to target specific demographics, interests, and behaviors, social media advertising allows you to get your message in front of the people who are most likely to be interested in what you have to offer. In this chapter, we'll explore the ins and outs of social media advertising, including how to create effective ads, target the right audience, and measure your success.

Understanding Social Media Advertising

Social media advertising is a form of online advertising that uses social media platforms to promote products, services, or brands. Rather than relying on organic reach, social media advertising allows you to pay for increased visibility and reach. There are a variety of ad formats available on different platforms, including sponsored posts, display ads, video ads, and more.

One of the key advantages of social media advertising is the ability to target specific audiences. Each platform has its own targeting options, allowing you to hone in on the people who are most likely to be interested in your brand. For example, you might target people based on their age, location, interests, behaviors, or even job title.

Creating Effective Ads

Creating effective social media ads requires a deep understanding of your target audience and what they're looking for. You need to craft a message that speaks directly to their needs and desires, and use visuals that capture their attention and engage them. Here are a few tips for creating effective social media ads:

1. Use eye-catching visuals: Social media platforms are highly visual, so you'll need to use visuals that are both eye-catching and relevant to your message. Consider using high-quality images, graphics, or videos that convey your message in a way that's visually engaging.

2. Keep it simple: Your message should be clear and concise, with a strong call to action that encourages people to take the next step. Avoid cluttering your ad with too much text or too

many visuals, as this can be overwhelming for viewers.

3. Be audience-focused: Remember that your ad is not about you – it's about your audience. Keep your message focused on their needs and desires, and use language that speaks directly to them.

Targeting Your Audience

To get the most out of your social media ads, you need to target the right audience. This means identifying the people who are most likely to be interested in what you have to offer, and tailoring your message to their needs and interests. Here are a few tips for targeting your audience effectively:

1. Use audience insights: Many social media platforms provide audience insights that allow you to understand your target audience better. Use this information to identify common interests, behaviors, and demographics, and tailor your message accordingly.

2. Refine your audience: As you run ads, pay attention to the performance metrics and adjust your targeting accordingly. If you notice that certain demographics or interests aren't

responding to your ads, you may need to refine your audience to focus on a more specific group.

3. Experiment with different audiences: Don't be afraid to experiment with different audience targeting options. Try targeting people based on different interests, behaviors, or demographics, and see which ones perform the best.

Social media advertising has become an increasingly important component of building a successful brand in the digital age. With the ability to reach a highly targeted audience and the ability to track and analyze results in real-time, social media advertising is an effective way to build your brand and reach new audiences. In this chapter, we will explore the benefits of social media advertising, how it works, and best practices for getting started.

The Benefits of Social Media Advertising

Social media advertising offers a number of benefits for building your brand and reaching new audiences. Some of the key benefits include:

Highly Targeted Audiences

Social media platforms like Facebook, Instagram, Twitter, and LinkedIn allow you to target specific audiences based on factors like age, gender, location, interests, and more. This means you can ensure your ads are being shown to the people most likely to be interested in your products or services.

Cost-Effective

Social media advertising can be a cost-effective way to reach a large audience. Compared to traditional advertising methods like television, radio, or print ads, social media advertising often requires a lower budget and can provide a higher return on investment.

Measurable Results

Social media advertising allows you to track and analyze the performance of your ads in real-time. This means you can adjust your strategy as needed to improve performance and ensure you are getting the best possible results.

How Social Media Advertising Works

Social media advertising works by allowing you to create ads that are displayed on social media platforms to a targeted audience. The process typically involves:

1. Choosing your platform: There are a number of social media platforms that offer advertising options, including Facebook, Instagram, Twitter, and LinkedIn. Choose the platform that is best suited to your brand and target audience.

2. Setting your budget: You can choose how much you want to spend on your advertising campaign, which will determine how often your ads are displayed and how many people they reach.

3. Creating your ad: This involves choosing the format of your ad, writing your copy, and selecting your images or videos.

4. Targeting your audience: You can choose specific demographics and interests to ensure your ads are being shown to the people most likely to be interested in your products or services.

5. Launching your ad: Once you have created your ad and set your targeting, you can launch your ad and start reaching your target audience.

Best Practices for Social Media Advertising

To get the most out of your social media advertising, it's important to follow some best practices. Some of the key best practices for social media advertising include:

Set Clear Objectives

Before you start your social media advertising campaign, it's important to set clear objectives. This could include goals like driving traffic to your website, increasing brand awareness, or generating leads. Having clear objectives will help you determine the best strategies for reaching your target audience and measuring your success.

Use Eye-Catching Visuals

Social media is a visual medium, which means your ads need to be eye-catching and visually appealing. This could include using high-quality images or videos, bold colors, and strong visual branding.

Be Concise

When it comes to writing your ad copy, it's important to be concise and get to the point quickly. Social media users have short attention spans, so you need to grab their attention and get your message across in just a few words.

Test and Adjust

One of the biggest benefits of social media advertising is the ability to track and analyze your results in real-time. This means you can test different strategies and adjust your approach as needed to improve your results.

In conclusion, social media advertising can be an effective way to build your brand and reach new audiences. By creating targeted ads, you can reach people who are more likely to be interested in your products or services. Paid ads allow you to increase your brand visibility, drive traffic to your website, and generate leads and sales.

However, it's important to approach social media advertising strategically. You should have a clear understanding of your target audience, choose the right platform for your goals, and create ads that are engaging and relevant. By measuring your results and making adjustments to your strategy, you can continually improve your social media advertising efforts and get the most out of your budget.

Remember that while paid ads can be effective, they are just one part of a comprehensive social media strategy. To truly build a strong brand, you need to engage with your audience, create valuable content, and build relationships through networking and collaborations. By combining all of these tactics, you can build a brand that resonates with your audience and drives long-term success.

Chapter 25

Building a Community

social media platforms have provided businesses with a powerful way to connect and engage with their audience. One of the keys to success on social media is building a strong and loyal community of fans and followers. In this chapter, we will explore the steps that businesses can take to build a community on social media and create a space where their fans and followers can connect, engage, and share.

1. Know your audience

The first step to building a community on social media is to know your audience. Understanding your target audience, their needs, interests, and pain points will help you create content that resonates with them and drives engagement. To get a better understanding of your audience, use analytics tools on social media platforms to track engagement metrics and demographics, conduct surveys or focus groups, and monitor feedback on social media.

2. Define your community

Once you know your audience, the next step is to define your community. A community is a group of people with shared interests or values, and your community should reflect your brand values and voice. Define the purpose of your community and what value it provides to your followers. This will help attract the right people and create a space where they feel welcome and engaged.

3. Create engaging content

To build a community on social media, you need to create engaging and shareable content. This can include posts, videos, images, and stories that speak to your audience's needs and interests. Use a mix of different types of content to keep your audience engaged and entertained. Consider collaborating with influencers or other brands to create content that is fun, informative, or inspiring.

4. Encourage user-generated content

One of the best ways to build a community on social media is to encourage user-generated content. This is content that your followers create and share on their own. Encouraging user-generated content can help build a sense of community and loyalty among your followers. Use hashtags, contests, and challenges to encourage your followers to share their own content and engage with your brand.

5. Respond to comments and messages

Engagement is a key component of building a community on social media. Responding to comments and messages in a timely and authentic way can help foster a sense of community and trust with your followers. Make sure to monitor your social media channels regularly and respond to all comments and messages, even negative ones. This will show your followers that you are listening and that their opinions and feedback matter to you.

6. Host events and meetups

Hosting events and meetups is a great way to build a strong community on social media. These events can be online or in-person and can range from live-streaming Q&A sessions to meetups at a local coffee shop. Hosting events and meetups will give your followers a chance to connect with you and other members of the community. This can help build a strong sense of community and loyalty around your brand.

7. Build a brand ambassador program

Another way to build a community on social media is to build a brand ambassador program. This is a program where you identify and work with your most loyal and engaged followers to help promote your brand. Brand ambassadors can help spread the word about your brand, share your content, and engage with other members of the community. They can also provide valuable feedback on your products or services.

In conclusion, building a community on social media is essential for businesses looking to establish a strong online presence and connect with their audience. To do this, businesses must understand their audience, create engaging content, encourage user-generated content, respond to comments and messages, host events and meetups, and build a brand ambassador program. With these strategies, businesses can create a space where their fans and followers can connect, engage, and share.

Chapter 26

Crisis Management

social media has become an essential part of building a brand and engaging with your audience. With the power to reach millions of people, it's a platform where businesses can grow their customer base, increase brand awareness, and promote products and services. However, it's not always sunshine and rainbows in the world of social media. Negative feedback, online criticism, and potential crises can all harm a brand's reputation, making it essential to have a plan in place for crisis management.

In this chapter, we'll discuss the importance of handling negative feedback and responding effectively. We'll cover the steps you need to take to turn negative feedback into an opportunity to build a better relationship with your audience.

Step 1: Monitor your brand mentions

One of the most important things you can do to prevent a crisis is to monitor your brand mentions. This involves keeping an eye on social media channels for any mentions of your brand, products, or services. By doing this, you can quickly identify any negative feedback or comments and respond promptly.

Several social media monitoring tools can help you track your brand mentions. These tools include Hootsuite, Mention, and Google Alerts. By using these tools, you can stay on top of what people are saying about your brand, giving you a chance to respond and manage any negative feedback before it gets out of hand.

Step 2: Respond promptly and appropriately

When you receive negative feedback or comments, it's essential to respond promptly and appropriately. This means addressing the issue at hand, acknowledging the problem, and providing a solution. A quick response shows that you care about your audience and are willing to take action to resolve their concerns.

It's crucial to handle negative feedback professionally and without becoming defensive or argumentative. Even if the comment is unjustified, it's important to remain calm and empathetic. Responding aggressively or sarcastically can make the situation worse and harm your brand's reputation.

Step 3: Apologize and offer a solution

When negative feedback is valid, it's important to take ownership of the situation, apologize, and offer a solution. An apology can go a long way in making the person feel heard and valued. It shows that you are committed to providing a positive experience for your customers and are willing to make things right.

Offering a solution can also help to ease the situation. This could be as simple as providing a discount or refund for a product or service. It's important to make the solution clear and specific to the issue at hand. By doing so, you can turn a negative experience into a positive one, building trust with your audience and increasing loyalty to your brand.

Step 4: Know when to take the conversation offline

There may be times when negative feedback or comments require more than a simple online response. In these cases, it's best to take the conversation offline. This could involve offering to speak with the person privately over email, phone, or a one-on-one meeting. This approach can help to resolve the issue and demonstrate that you take customer feedback seriously.

Step 5: Learn from the experience

Negative feedback can be a valuable learning experience. It provides insight into areas of your business that need improvement, allowing you to make changes and prevent similar issues from happening in the future. By analyzing the feedback and understanding the root cause of the problem, you can make changes that benefit both your business and your customers.

Conclusion

Handling negative feedback and crises is an essential part of building a successful brand on social media. By monitoring your brand mentions, responding promptly and appropriately, offering a solution, knowing when to take the conversation offline, and learning from the experience, you can turn negative feedback into a positive experience. By doing so, you'll build trust and loyalty with your audience and establish a positive reputation for your brand.

Chapter 27

Brand Consistency

In today's crowded digital landscape, it's more important than ever to have a strong and consistent brand presence across all channels. This means ensuring that your brand identity, messaging, and visual elements are consistent and cohesive no matter where your audience encounters your brand.

Brand consistency is important for several reasons. First, it helps to build brand recognition and awareness. If your branding is inconsistent, it can be difficult for your audience to recognize and remember your brand, leading to confusion and missed opportunities. Second, a consistent brand helps to build trust and credibility with your audience. If your messaging is all over the place or your visual identity is constantly changing, it can create a sense of unreliability or lack of professionalism.

Here are some key steps to building and maintaining brand consistency across all your channels:

1. Develop your brand guidelines: Your brand guidelines are a set of rules and guidelines that outline how your brand should be presented

across all channels. This can include elements such as your brand's tone of voice, visual identity, logo usage, and more. Your brand guidelines should be easily accessible and regularly updated as your brand evolves.

2. Use the same visual elements: Your brand's visual identity should be consistent across all channels, including your website, social media, and any marketing materials. This includes using the same logo, colors, typography, and imagery. Make sure your brand's visuals are recognizable and distinct to help your brand stand out from competitors.

3. Keep your messaging consistent: Your brand's messaging should also be consistent across all channels. This means using the same tone of voice and messaging points across all marketing materials and channels. Your messaging should also reflect your brand values and be tailored to your target audience.

4. Train your team: Make sure your team members are all on the same page when it comes to your brand's guidelines and messaging. This can include providing regular training on your brand's values, messaging, and visual identity,

as well as ensuring that everyone has access to your brand guidelines.

5. Monitor and adapt: Regularly monitor your brand's performance and adapt your branding and messaging as needed. This can include updating your brand guidelines or making changes to your visual identity to better resonate with your target audience.

By following these key steps, you can ensure that your brand is consistent and recognizable across all channels. This can help to build trust and credibility with your audience and set your brand apart from competitors.

Chapter 28

Repurposing Content

As a content creator, you spend a lot of time and effort creating quality content that engages your audience and promotes your brand. However, it can be challenging to continually come up with new content ideas, especially when you're managing multiple social media platforms. Repurposing content is an effective way to make the most out of your existing content and maximize its reach across various platforms.

Repurposing content means taking a piece of content that you've already created and adapting it for use on a different platform or in a different format. It's an excellent strategy for reaching a broader audience and saving time and resources while still providing valuable content to your followers.

Here are some tips to help you repurpose your content effectively:

1. Start with a Content Audit

Before you begin repurposing your content, it's essential to conduct a content audit to identify your most successful content pieces. Look at your website analytics, social media metrics, and other relevant data to see which pieces of content have performed the best in terms of engagement and reach.

Once you've identified your top-performing pieces of content, you can begin repurposing them for use on other platforms.

2. Consider Different Formats

When repurposing your content, consider different formats that might be appropriate for different platforms. For example, you could turn a blog post into an infographic or a podcast episode into a video. By adapting your content for different formats, you can reach a wider audience and provide valuable content in a way that suits their preferences.

3. Repurpose Across Different Platforms

Once you've repurposed your content into different formats, you can then post it on various platforms. For example, if you've created a video, you can post it on YouTube, share it on Facebook, and embed it on your website. By doing this, you can reach a broader audience and maximize the impact of your content.

4. Tailor Your Content for Each Platform

It's crucial to tailor your content for each platform you're using. While it's okay to repurpose content across platforms, you need to adapt it to suit the audience and context of each platform. For example, your LinkedIn audience may prefer more professional content, while your Instagram followers may respond better to visually appealing content.

5. Keep Your Branding Consistent

When repurposing your content, ensure that your branding remains consistent across all platforms. This means using the same logo, color scheme, and fonts to help your followers recognize your brand quickly. Consistency is key to building brand recognition and increasing brand loyalty.

6. Use Automation Tools

Repurposing content can be a time-consuming process. To save time and resources, consider using automation tools that allow you to schedule your content for posting across different platforms. Tools like Hootsuite and Buffer are great options for scheduling posts in advance, so you can focus on creating new content.

In conclusion, repurposing content is an effective way to maximize the impact of your existing content while saving time and resources. By repurposing content across different platforms and formats, you can reach a wider audience and provide valuable content in a way that suits their preferences. Remember to tailor your content for each platform, keep your branding consistent, and use automation tools to streamline the process. By following these tips, you'll be able to create a content strategy that engages your audience and promotes your brand effectively.

Chapter 29

Outsourcing

In today's digital age, there are countless opportunities for businesses to build their brands and reach new audiences through social media and digital marketing. However, with so many different channels and strategies available, it can be overwhelming for business owners to know where to focus their efforts. One way to ensure you are making the most of your time and resources is by outsourcing certain tasks to qualified professionals. In this chapter, we will discuss the benefits of outsourcing and how it can help your brand thrive.

First and foremost, outsourcing allows you to focus on what you do best - running your business. When you hire a professional to handle tasks such as social media management, content creation, or email marketing, you are freeing up your own time to focus on the core aspects of your business. This not only ensures that you are maximizing your own strengths, but it also allows you to work more efficiently and effectively.

Outsourcing also provides you with access to a wide range of expertise and experience. When you hire a professional to handle a specific task, you are benefiting from their specialized knowledge and skills. For example, if you hire a social media manager, they will be well-versed in the latest trends and strategies for building your brand on social media. This means that you are more likely to see results, as you are working with someone who knows how to get the job done.

Another benefit of outsourcing is that it can save you money in the long run. While it may seem like hiring a professional is more expensive than handling tasks in-house, it is important to consider the long-term cost savings. For example, if you hire a professional to manage your social media channels, they will be able to create more effective and targeted content that is more likely to engage your audience. This means that you will see better results and a higher return on investment.

When outsourcing tasks, it is important to find the right person or team for the job. You should look for someone who has a track record of success in the specific area you are looking to outsource. For example, if you are looking for someone to handle your email marketing campaigns, you should look for someone who has experience in creating effective email marketing campaigns that drive results. You should also look for someone who has good communication skills and is responsive to your needs and feedback.

It is also important to establish clear expectations and guidelines for the person or team you are outsourcing to. This includes outlining the specific tasks and responsibilities they will be handling, as well as any deadlines or goals you have in mind. You should also be clear about your brand voice and style, so that the person or team you are outsourcing to can create content that is consistent with your brand.

When it comes to outsourcing, there are a few areas that are particularly well-suited for delegating to professionals. One of these is social media management. Social media is a crucial part of any digital marketing strategy, but it can also be time-consuming and complex to manage. Hiring a social media manager can help ensure that your channels are regularly updated with engaging content that resonates with your audience.

Another area that is well-suited for outsourcing is content creation. Whether you need blog posts, social media content, or email marketing campaigns, creating high-quality and engaging content is essential for building your brand and reaching new audiences. By hiring a content creator, you can ensure that your content is well-written, targeted, and effective at driving engagement.

Finally, email marketing is another area that can benefit from outsourcing. Email marketing is an incredibly effective way to reach your audience and drive sales, but it can also be time-consuming to create and manage campaigns. By hiring an email marketing specialist, you can ensure that your campaigns are well-crafted and effective at driving results.

conclusion, outsourcing can be a valuable tool for businesses looking to grow and expand their brand. By delegating tasks to skilled professionals, business owners can free up their time and energy to focus on their core competencies and driving the success of their brand.

Whether it's outsourcing content creation, social media management, or administrative tasks, there are a wide variety of outsourcing options available to businesses of all sizes. By working with reputable freelancers or outsourcing companies, businesses can tap into a wealth of expertise and experience that can help them stay ahead of the curve and thrive in an increasingly competitive market.

Of course, outsourcing is not a one-size-fits-all solution, and it's important for business owners to carefully evaluate their needs and goals before deciding which tasks to delegate and which professionals to work with. However, with the right approach and a clear understanding of the benefits and potential pitfalls of outsourcing, businesses can leverage this powerful tool to achieve their brand's full potential and drive long-term success.

Chapter 30

Building a Team

Building a successful brand requires a lot of time, effort, and energy. While it may be possible to do everything yourself at the beginning, as your brand grows, you will likely need to build a team to support your efforts. Hiring a team can help you take your brand to the next level, but it also comes with its own set of challenges.

In this chapter, we will explore the benefits of building a team for your brand, how to find the right team members, and how to manage them effectively.

Benefits of Building a Team

One of the biggest benefits of building a team is that it allows you to scale your brand. As your brand grows, you will likely need more people to help you manage different aspects of your business, such as marketing, customer service, and product development. A team can also help you to free up time and energy so you can focus on the areas of your business where you excel.

Another benefit of building a team is that it can help you to bring in new perspectives and ideas. When you work with a group of people, you get to draw on their unique experiences and skillsets. This can be invaluable in helping you to solve problems and come up with new ideas.

Finding the Right Team Members

Finding the right team members can be a challenge, but it is critical to the success of your brand. The first step is to identify the roles that you need to fill. Consider the areas of your business where you need the most help and create job descriptions that outline the responsibilities and qualifications required for each role.

Once you have a clear idea of the roles you need to fill, you can begin the recruitment process. There are a number of ways to find potential team members, including job boards, social media, and referrals. It's important to be clear about your expectations and to look for candidates who are a good fit for your brand culture.

When you are reviewing resumes and conducting interviews, be sure to ask questions that will help you to assess a candidate's skills, experience, and fit for your team. You may also want to consider having candidates complete skills tests or work on a project to see how they would perform in the role.

Managing Your Team

Managing a team can be challenging, but it is essential to the success of your brand. One of the keys to effective management is to be clear about your expectations and to provide your team with the resources and support they need to do their job effectively.

It's also important to communicate regularly with your team members. This can include regular check-ins, team meetings, and feedback sessions. When giving feedback, be sure to focus on specific behaviors and outcomes rather than making personal attacks or generalizations.

Another key to effective management is to create a culture of trust and transparency. This means being honest with your team members about your expectations, the challenges you are facing, and the decisions you are making. When your team members trust you and feel like they are part of a transparent and collaborative culture, they will be more likely to be engaged and committed to your brand.

Conclusion

Building a team is an important step in growing your brand and taking it to the next level. When done effectively, it can help you to scale your business, bring in new perspectives and ideas, and free up your time and energy to focus on the areas of your business where you excel.

Finding the right team members and managing them effectively can be challenging, but by being clear about your expectations, communicating regularly, and creating a culture of trust and transparency, you can set your team up for success.

Chapter 31

Brand Partnerships

Building a brand is no easy task. It takes time, effort, and resources to develop a strong brand identity that resonates with your target audience. While it's essential to focus on building your brand and establishing a unique identity, you shouldn't do it alone. There is strength in numbers, and sometimes the best way to grow your brand is to collaborate with other brands.

Brand partnerships can be an incredibly powerful tool for building your brand and reaching new audiences. By working with other brands, you can leverage each other's strengths and create something that is greater than the sum of its parts. In this chapter, we'll explore the benefits of brand partnerships and offer tips on how to create successful collaborations.

Benefits of Brand Partnerships

There are many benefits to partnering with another brand. One of the most significant advantages is that it can help you reach new audiences. By working with a brand that already has an established following, you can introduce your brand to a whole new group of people. In addition, brand partnerships can help you build credibility and establish trust with your target audience. When you align yourself with a brand that your target audience already trusts, it can help you build trust by association.

Another significant advantage of brand partnerships is that they can help you access new resources. For example, if you're a small business, partnering with a larger brand can give you access to resources that you wouldn't have otherwise. This could include things like funding, marketing, and distribution.

Creating Successful Brand Partnerships

The key to creating successful brand partnerships is to find brands that are complementary to yours. This means looking for brands that have similar values and target the same or similar audiences. When you partner with a brand that complements your own, it's easier to create something that is greater than the sum of its parts.

When you're looking for potential brand partners, make sure to do your research. Look at their brand values, target audience, and marketing strategy to see if they align with your own. You can also look at their social media channels to see how they engage with their followers and what kind of content they create.

Once you've identified potential brand partners, it's essential to reach out to them and start building a relationship. The first step is to introduce yourself and your brand and explain why you think a partnership would be beneficial. It's important to be clear about your goals and what you hope to achieve through the partnership.

It's also essential to be open and flexible when it comes to creating a partnership. You may need to compromise and find a middle ground that works for both brands. This could include co-creating content, offering promotions, or collaborating on events.

Case Study: Nike and Apple

One of the most famous brand partnerships is between Nike and Apple. In 2006, the two brands partnered to create Nike+, a platform that allowed runners to track their progress using an iPod and Nike shoes. The partnership was a huge success, with Nike and Apple both benefiting from the collaboration.

The partnership was successful because it was a natural fit. Both brands were known for their commitment to innovation and their focus on empowering their customers. By working together, they were able to create something that aligned with their shared values and helped both brands reach new audiences.

Conclusion

Brand partnerships can be an incredibly powerful tool for building your brand and reaching new audiences. By working with other brands, you can leverage each other's strengths and create something that is greater than the sum of its parts. When creating a brand partnership, it's essential to find brands that are complementary to your own, and to be open and flexible when it comes to creating a partnership.

Giving Back

As businesses continue to expand their reach and impact on society, there is a growing need for them to be more socially responsible. Consumers are increasingly aware of the impact of their actions on the environment, society, and their well-being. Therefore, building a socially responsible brand is not only good for the world but also good for business.

In this chapter, we'll explore what it means to build a socially responsible brand, why it's important, and how to get started.

What is a Socially Responsible Brand?

A socially responsible brand is one that takes into account the social and environmental impact of its business activities. It recognizes that it has a responsibility to the world around it and actively works to improve the well-being of its stakeholders, including its employees, customers, and the wider community.

Socially responsible brands also consider the impact of their products or services on the environment, seeking to reduce waste, emissions, and other negative environmental effects. They recognize that their actions have consequences and strive to make a positive impact on the world.

Why is Social Responsibility Important?

Building a socially responsible brand is not only a moral imperative but also a business advantage. Consumers are increasingly aware of the impact of their choices and are more likely to choose brands that align with their values. According to a recent study, 64% of consumers worldwide will buy or boycott a brand based on its social or political stance.

In addition, socially responsible brands tend to attract and retain top talent. Employees are more likely to be engaged and committed to their work when they feel that their company is making a positive impact on the world.

Finally, being socially responsible can help businesses to mitigate risks and avoid negative publicity. By actively working to address social and environmental issues, brands can build trust and credibility with their stakeholders, reducing the risk of negative press or public backlash.

Getting Started with Social Responsibility

Building a socially responsible brand requires a commitment to social and environmental sustainability. Here are some steps to get started:

1. Define Your Values and Goals

To build a socially responsible brand, it's essential to define your values and goals. This involves understanding the social and environmental impact of your business and identifying areas where you can make a positive difference. It also requires setting specific goals and metrics to measure progress.

2. Engage Your Stakeholders

Engaging with your stakeholders is key to building a socially responsible brand. This includes employees, customers, suppliers, and the wider community. Seek feedback and input from these groups to understand their needs and expectations and incorporate their feedback into your social responsibility strategy.

3. Develop a Social Responsibility Strategy

Develop a comprehensive social responsibility strategy that outlines your goals, initiatives, and metrics for success. This should include specific targets for reducing waste, emissions, and other environmental impacts, as well as programs to support employees and the wider community.

4. Incorporate Social Responsibility into Your
   Business Operations

Integrate social responsibility into your day-to-day business operations. This includes developing policies and procedures to reduce waste, emissions, and other environmental impacts, as well as supporting employee well-being and community development.

5. Communicate Your Commitment

Communicate your commitment to social responsibility through your marketing and communication channels. This includes your website, social media, and other promotional materials. Be transparent about your goals, initiatives, and progress towards achieving them.

6. Measure and Monitor Progress

Finally, it's essential to measure and monitor your progress towards achieving your social responsibility goals. Use metrics and analytics to track your impact on the environment, society, and your stakeholders. This will help you to identify areas for improvement and make necessary adjustments to your strategy.

conclusion, building a socially responsible brand is no longer an option, but rather a necessity for any business that wants to thrive in today's world. Consumers have become more conscious of the impact of their purchasing decisions, and they now expect businesses to be accountable for their actions and to contribute to making the world a better place.

By giving back to society, businesses can make a positive impact on the world while also strengthening their brand. Philanthropic initiatives, sustainability efforts, and ethical practices not only benefit society but also enhance a brand's reputation, customer loyalty, and overall success.

When it comes to building a socially responsible brand, there are various approaches that businesses can take. Some may choose to partner with nonprofit organizations to support a specific cause, while others may focus on sustainable practices to minimize their environmental footprint. Whatever approach a business takes, it's important to make sure that it aligns with the brand's values and mission.

Ultimately, a socially responsible brand is one that is committed to creating a better world, not just for its customers and shareholders but for all members of society. By giving back, businesses can foster a sense of purpose and make a positive impact on the world, while also building a strong and successful brand.

Chapter 33

Reputation Management

In today's digital age, it's important for businesses and individuals alike to maintain a positive reputation online. With the ease of access to information and social media platforms, people have more ways to communicate and share their experiences with others. This can make or break a brand's reputation, making it important to stay on top of what people are saying about you online. In this chapter, we'll discuss how to build and maintain a positive reputation online through reputation management.

What is Reputation Management? Reputation management refers to the process of monitoring and controlling what people are saying about your brand online. This involves analyzing the online feedback, addressing negative feedback, and encouraging positive feedback. Your online reputation can be influenced by a variety of factors, such as customer reviews, news articles, social media posts, and more. By monitoring these channels, you can identify negative comments and proactively take action to address them.

Why Reputation Management is Important A positive reputation is critical to the success of any business. Your reputation is what makes you stand out from the competition and is what customers use to make purchasing decisions. Negative feedback can impact your sales, and it's crucial to have a solid reputation management strategy in place to prevent this from happening. Positive feedback, on the other hand, can lead to increased sales and customer loyalty. By actively managing your online reputation, you can stay ahead of the competition and ensure long-term success for your brand.

Steps to Building and Maintaining a Positive Reputation

1. Monitor Your Online Presence To effectively manage your reputation, you need to know what people are saying about your brand online. Set up Google Alerts for your brand, monitor social media channels, and keep track of any news articles that mention your business. By staying informed, you can quickly identify any negative feedback and take steps to address it.

2. Respond to Negative Feedback When negative feedback is posted online, it's important to address it promptly and professionally.

Respond to the negative feedback with empathy, and do everything you can to resolve the issue. This shows that you care about your customers and their experiences and can help turn a negative situation into a positive one.

3. Encourage Positive Feedback Encourage your customers to leave positive feedback by making it easy for them to do so. Add review widgets to your website and social media pages, and include a call-to-action in your email communications asking for feedback. Respond to positive feedback and show appreciation for your customers' support.

4. Build Relationships with Your Customers Building strong relationships with your customers is key to maintaining a positive reputation. Engage with them on social media, respond to their comments and messages, and show that you value their input. By building a strong connection with your customers, you can create a loyal customer base that will be more likely to leave positive feedback.

5. Stay Transparent and Authentic In the age of social media, transparency and authenticity are key to building and maintaining a positive reputation. Be honest about your business

practices, admit when you make a mistake, and show your customers that you are constantly striving to improve. This creates a sense of trust and loyalty among your customers.

6. Be Proactive Don't wait for negative feedback to pop up online before taking action. Be proactive in managing your reputation by regularly checking your online channels and addressing any issues before they become larger problems. This can help you stay ahead of the game and prevent any negative feedback from impacting your brand.

Here are some tips for building and maintaining a positive reputation online:

1. Monitor Your Reputation

The first step in managing your reputation is to know what people are saying about your brand online. This can be done by setting up Google Alerts or using social listening tools that will notify you when your brand is mentioned on social media, review sites, or other online platforms. By monitoring your reputation, you can quickly address any negative feedback or reviews and take steps to prevent similar issues from happening in the future.

2. Respond to Feedback and Reviews

When you receive feedback or reviews, it's essential to respond quickly and professionally. Thank customers for their feedback, address any concerns they have, and offer a solution if possible. By showing that you care about your customers and their experiences, you can turn a negative situation into a positive one.

4. Respond to negative feedback

Negative feedback is inevitable, and it's important to have a plan in place for how to respond to it. The way you handle negative feedback can make all the difference in how your brand is perceived by your audience. When responding to negative feedback, keep these tips in mind:

- Respond promptly: Address the issue as soon as possible to prevent it from escalating.

- Acknowledge the concern: Show empathy and understanding for the customer's issue or complaint.

- Take responsibility: If your brand made a mistake, own up to it and take steps to make it right.

- Offer a solution: Offer a solution or make a plan to resolve the issue.

- Keep it professional: Stay professional and avoid engaging in arguments or negativity.

5. Monitor your online presence

Keeping a close eye on your online presence is crucial to reputation management. This means monitoring social media channels, search engine results, review sites, and other areas where your brand is mentioned online. Use tools like Google Alerts, Hootsuite, and Sprout Social to monitor online mentions and respond promptly to any negative feedback or mentions. It's also important to regularly check review sites like Yelp and TripAdvisor to address any negative reviews and show your commitment to customer satisfaction.

6. Engage in online reputation management

Online reputation management involves actively building and maintaining a positive online reputation for your brand. This can be done through tactics such as:

- Publishing high-quality, informative content that highlights your brand's strengths and expertise.

- Encouraging positive reviews and feedback from satisfied customers.

- Responding promptly and professionally to negative feedback and complaints.

- Monitoring and addressing any negative content or reviews that appear online.

- Building a strong social media presence and engaging with your audience in a positive way.

By actively engaging in online reputation management, you can build and maintain a positive online reputation for your brand, which can lead to increased trust, loyalty, and sales.

In conclusion, reputation management is essential for building and maintaining a positive online presence for your brand. By being proactive, responding promptly to negative feedback, and actively monitoring and managing your online reputation, you can build trust with your audience and establish your brand as a leader in your industry.

Chapter 34

Building Your Personal Brand as a Public Figure

In today's age of social media, being a public figure is not just limited to actors and politicians. Anyone with a following and a message can be considered a public figure, and with that comes the responsibility of building and maintaining a personal brand.

A personal brand is how you are perceived by others, and it can have a significant impact on your success as a public figure. In this chapter, we will discuss the steps you can take to create and cultivate a strong personal brand.

1. Define Your Message Before you can create a personal brand, you need to know what you want to be known for. What is your message? What is your passion? What do you want to achieve? Once you have a clear idea of your message, you can begin to build your brand around it.

2. Identify Your Target Audience To build a successful personal brand, you need to know

who you are trying to reach. Identify your target audience and create content that resonates with them. Knowing your audience will help you create content that speaks directly to them, and will help you build a loyal following.

3. Be Authentic Your personal brand is a reflection of who you are, so it is important to be authentic. Don't try to be someone you're not, and don't pretend to be interested in things that you're not. Be true to yourself, and your audience will appreciate it.

4. Use Social Media Strategically Social media is a powerful tool for building a personal brand. Use it strategically to reach your target audience, and to build a loyal following. Create content that is both interesting and valuable, and engage with your audience regularly.

5. Collaborate with Others Collaborating with other public figures can help you expand your reach and build your personal brand. Identify other influencers or celebrities in your industry, and reach out to them to collaborate on a project. This can help you reach a new audience and establish yourself as an authority in your field.

6. Be Consistent Consistency is key when it comes to building a personal brand. You need to be consistent in the way you present yourself and in the content you create. If you're inconsistent, your audience will become confused and disengaged.

7. Engage with Your Audience Engaging with your audience is important for building a personal brand. Respond to comments and messages, and take the time to connect with your followers. This will help you build a loyal following and establish yourself as a thought leader in your industry.

8. Monitor Your Reputation As a public figure, your reputation is everything. It is important to monitor your reputation online, and to take action if you receive negative feedback. Responding to negative feedback in a positive and constructive way can help you build a positive reputation and show your audience that you care about their opinions.

9. Be Open to Change Your personal brand is not set in stone. It can and will evolve over time. Be open to change, and be willing to pivot your brand if necessary. This will help you stay relevant and keep your audience engaged.

In conclusion, building a personal brand as a public figure is crucial to your success. By defining your message, identifying your target audience, being authentic, using social media strategically, collaborating with others, being consistent, engaging with your audience, monitoring your reputation, and being open to change, you can create a personal brand that resonates with your audience and helps you achieve your goals.

Chapter 35

Building Your Personal Brand as an Entrepreneur

As an entrepreneur, you are the face of your business, and your personal brand is critical to your company's success. Your personal brand is what sets you apart from your competitors, and it is what attracts customers to your business. In this chapter, we will discuss the importance of personal branding for entrepreneurs and provide tips on how to build a strong personal brand that aligns with your business.

Why Personal Branding is Important for Entrepreneurs

As an entrepreneur, your personal brand is your most valuable asset. People do business with people they know, like, and trust. By creating a strong personal brand, you can build relationships with potential customers, establish yourself as an expert in your field, and attract new business opportunities. Your personal brand is what sets you apart from your competitors and gives your customers a reason to choose you over others.

Steps to Building Your Personal Brand as an Entrepreneur

1. Define your brand

The first step in building your personal brand is to define who you are and what you stand for. Take some time to think about your values, strengths, and skills. What do you want to be known for? What makes you unique? Once you have a clear idea of who you are, you can start to build a personal brand that reflects your identity.

2. Identify your audience

Your personal brand should be designed to appeal to your target audience. Who are you trying to reach? What are their needs and preferences? By understanding your audience, you can tailor your messaging to resonate with them.

3. Create a brand story

Your brand story is the narrative that defines your personal brand. It should communicate who you are, what you stand for, and what makes you unique. Your brand story should be compelling, memorable, and authentic. It should also align with your business's mission and values.

4. Develop your online presence

In today's digital age, your online presence is critical to your personal brand. Make sure your website, social media profiles, and other online platforms reflect your brand identity. Consistency is key, so use the same colors, fonts, and tone of voice across all channels.

5. Publish content

Creating and publishing content is a great way to establish yourself as an expert in your field. Consider starting a blog, hosting a podcast, or writing a book. Share your content on social media and other online platforms to reach a wider audience.

6. Attend networking events

Networking is an important part of building your personal brand. Attend industry events, conferences, and trade shows to meet other professionals in your field. Share your knowledge and expertise, and build relationships with potential customers and partners.

7. Partner with other brands

Partnering with other brands can help to extend your reach and build your credibility. Look for opportunities to collaborate with other entrepreneurs or businesses in your industry. You can co-create content, host events together, or cross-promote each other's products or services.

Building a personal brand as an entrepreneur takes time and effort, but the rewards can be significant. By creating a strong personal brand, you can establish yourself as an expert in your field, attract new business opportunities, and build a loyal customer base. Remember to stay true to your values and personality, and always strive to provide value to your audience.

Chapter 36

Building Your Personal Brand as a Professional

In today's competitive job market, establishing a strong personal brand as a professional is essential for career success. Building a personal brand can help you stand out from other professionals and make a lasting impression on potential employers or clients. In this chapter, we will explore the key steps to building a personal brand as an expert in your field.

1. Define Your Brand Identity

The first step in building a personal brand is to define your brand identity. Your brand identity is the image that you want to project to the world. It encompasses your unique strengths, values, and personality traits. Defining your brand identity requires self-reflection and an honest assessment of your skills, experiences, and accomplishments.

To start, ask yourself the following questions:

- What are my core strengths and skills?

- What are my unique experiences and accomplishments?

- What values do I embody?

- What is my personality like?

- What is my overall vision for my career?

Use your answers to these questions to create a personal brand statement. Your personal brand statement should be a concise summary of who you are, what you do, and what you stand for.

2. Develop Your Online Presence

In today's digital age, having a strong online presence is critical to building a personal brand as a professional. Your online presence can include your personal website, social media profiles, and professional networking sites.

When developing your online presence, it is important to keep your personal brand in mind. Ensure that your online persona aligns with your personal brand statement. Use high-quality images and content that reflect your expertise and professionalism.

3. Create Valuable Content

Creating valuable content is an effective way to showcase your expertise and build your personal brand as a professional. Consider starting a blog, publishing articles on LinkedIn, or producing videos on YouTube. You can also share your knowledge through speaking engagements or by hosting webinars.

When creating content, focus on providing value to your audience. Share your knowledge and insights on topics related to your field. Engage with your audience and encourage feedback and discussion.

4. Build a Professional Network

Building a professional network is an important step in building a personal brand as a professional. Your professional network can help you gain exposure, create opportunities, and build your reputation.

Start by attending networking events and joining professional organizations related to your field. Connect with other professionals in your industry and build relationships with them. You can also use social media to expand your network by connecting with professionals in your field.

5. Establish Yourself as an Expert

Establishing yourself as an expert in your field is a key aspect of building a personal brand as a professional. Look for opportunities to share your knowledge and experience. Consider offering to speak at industry events, write articles for industry publications, or serve as a mentor to others.

By positioning yourself as an expert, you can build your reputation and establish yourself as a thought leader in your field. This can lead to new opportunities and help you stand out from other professionals.

In conclusion, building a personal brand as a professional requires a strategic approach. It requires self-reflection, a strong online presence, valuable content, a professional network, and a reputation as an expert in your field. By following these steps, you can build a personal brand that reflects your unique skills, values, and personality traits, and position yourself for success in your career.

Chapter 37

Building Your Personal Brand as a Creative

As a creative professional, building a personal brand is crucial to your success. Your brand represents your values, your skills, and your unique style, and it is what sets you apart from other creatives. Creating a strong personal brand can help you attract more clients, gain a larger following, and ultimately lead to more opportunities to showcase your work. In this chapter, we'll explore the steps you can take to build a personal brand as an artist, writer, or musician.

1. Define Your Unique Voice

The first step in building a personal brand as a creative is to define your unique voice. Your voice is what makes your work stand out from others in your field. Take some time to reflect on your strengths, your values, and what sets you apart from others. Use this reflection to create a personal brand statement that sums up your brand in a few words. This statement should be a clear and concise representation of who you are and what you do.

2. Create a Consistent Brand Image

Once you've defined your unique voice, it's time to create a consistent brand image. Your brand image is the visual representation of your personal brand. It includes your logo, color scheme, and other visual elements that are associated with your brand. To create a consistent brand image, it's important to choose colors and fonts that reflect your personality and your brand's voice. Use these elements consistently across all your marketing materials, including your website, social media profiles, and any other promotional materials.

3. Build a Strong Online Presence

As a creative professional, having a strong online presence is key to building your personal brand. Start by creating a website that showcases your work and highlights your unique style. Make sure your website is easy to navigate and features high-quality images of your work. Consider starting a blog to share your thoughts and insights about your creative process, or create video content to showcase your work.

In addition to your website, it's important to have a strong presence on social media. Choose social media platforms that are popular in your industry, and focus on building a following by sharing your work, engaging with your audience, and sharing insights about your creative process.

4. Network with Other Creatives

Networking with other creatives is a great way to build your personal brand and expand your opportunities. Attend industry events, join professional organizations, and connect with other creatives online. Building relationships with other creatives can lead to collaborations, joint projects, and other opportunities to showcase your work.

5. Showcase Your Expertise

As a creative professional, you have unique skills and expertise that set you apart from others in your field. Showcase your expertise by offering workshops, webinars, or other educational content to share your knowledge with others. By sharing your knowledge, you establish yourself as an expert in your field and build trust with your audience.

6. Stay Authentic

Finally, it's important to stay authentic and true to yourself as you build your personal brand. Your personal brand is a reflection of who you are, so it's important to stay true to your values and your unique style. Don't try to imitate others or change who you are to fit in. Authenticity is key to building a strong personal brand that resonates with your audience.

In conclusion, building a personal brand as a creative professional takes time and effort, but it's well worth it. By defining your unique voice, creating a consistent brand image, building a strong online presence, networking with other creatives, showcasing your expertise, and staying authentic, you can build a personal brand that sets you apart from others in your field and helps you attract more opportunities to showcase your work.

Chapter 38

Building Your Personal Brand as a Service Provider

As a consultant or coach, building a personal brand is essential to growing your business and gaining credibility in your field. Your personal brand represents your reputation, values, and unique expertise that sets you apart from your competitors. It also helps potential clients to understand who you are and what you can offer them.

In this chapter, we will discuss the steps you can take to build your personal brand as a service provider, from identifying your unique strengths to developing a consistent message across all your marketing channels.

Identify Your Unique Strengths

To create a strong personal brand, you need to identify your unique strengths and what sets you apart from other consultants or coaches in your field. This could be your years of experience, specialized expertise, or a unique methodology you've developed.

Start by conducting a personal inventory of your skills, experience, and areas of expertise. Think about your strengths, your passions, and what sets you apart from your competition. Consider what problems your potential clients are facing and how you can solve them.

Once you've identified your unique strengths, make sure to communicate them clearly in all of your marketing materials, including your website, social media, and other channels.

Develop a Consistent Message

Your personal brand message is the core message you want to convey to potential clients about who you are and what you do. It should be consistent across all your marketing channels, including your website, social media, and email marketing.

When developing your brand message, focus on your unique strengths and the value you provide to your clients. Make sure it's clear, concise, and easy to understand. Avoid using jargon or technical language that may confuse your audience.

When crafting your message, consider your target audience and what they need from you. Speak directly to them and address their pain points, showing how you can solve their problems.

Create a Strong Online Presence

In today's digital age, having a strong online presence is essential for building your personal brand as a service provider. Start by creating a professional website that showcases your experience, expertise, and services. Your website should also include testimonials from satisfied clients and contact information, making it easy for potential clients to reach out to you.

In addition to your website, social media is another key component of your online presence. Choose the social media platforms that are most relevant to your target audience, such as LinkedIn, Twitter, or Facebook. Make sure to post regularly and engage with your audience to build relationships and increase your visibility.

Consider creating and publishing content, such as blog posts, videos, or podcasts, to showcase your expertise and provide value to your audience. This can help establish you as a thought leader in your field and increase your credibility.

Network and Build Relationships

Networking and building relationships are critical to building your personal brand as a service provider. Attend industry events and conferences to meet other professionals in your field and potential clients. Consider joining industry associations or organizations and actively participate in their activities.

In addition to offline networking, online networking can also be an effective way to build relationships. Connect with other professionals and potential clients on social media and engage with them through comments, likes, and shares. Consider reaching out to influencers or thought leaders in your industry to see if they're interested in collaborating or featuring your work.

Deliver Excellent Service

Ultimately, your personal brand is built on the quality of service you provide to your clients. Delivering excellent service can lead to positive word-of-mouth referrals and repeat business.

Make sure to listen to your clients and understand their needs. Provide a personalized experience and always exceed their expectations. Act with integrity and ensure that your clients feel valued and appreciated.

As a service provider, building a personal brand can be the key to attracting new clients and growing your business. Whether you're a consultant, coach, or another type of service provider, your personal brand is an important part of your marketing strategy. Your personal brand is what sets you apart from your competitors and helps potential clients connect with you on a personal level. In this chapter, we'll explore how to build your personal brand as a service provider and attract the right clients.

1. Define Your Unique Value Proposition

As a service provider, it's essential to define your unique value proposition. What makes you different from your competitors? What is your specialty? What are your strengths and skills? These questions can help you identify your unique value proposition, which is what you can offer to your clients that no one else can. This will be the foundation of your personal brand.

2. Develop Your Brand Identity

Once you have defined your unique value proposition, it's time to develop your brand identity. This includes your brand name, logo, colors, fonts, and other visual elements. Your brand identity should be consistent across all of your marketing materials, from your website to your social media profiles.

3. Create Your Personal Brand Story

Your personal brand story is the story of how you got to where you are today. It should be authentic and connect with your target audience. Your personal brand story should highlight your unique value proposition and the value you can bring to your clients.

4. Establish Yourself as an Expert

Establishing yourself as an expert in your field is essential to building your personal brand as a service provider. This can be done by publishing articles, speaking at conferences, and participating in online communities. You can also offer free webinars or create online courses to showcase your expertise and attract potential clients.

5. Leverage Testimonials and Referrals

As a service provider, testimonials and referrals are crucial to building your personal brand. When a satisfied client provides a positive testimonial or refers you to someone else, it can be a powerful marketing tool. Be sure to ask for testimonials and referrals from satisfied clients and showcase them on your website and social media profiles.

6. Network and Collaborate

Networking and collaboration can be powerful tools for building your personal brand as a service provider. Attend industry events, join online communities, and seek out collaboration opportunities with other service providers in your field. This can help you establish yourself as a thought leader and increase your visibility in your industry.

7. Be Authentic and Consistent

Finally, it's important to be authentic and consistent in your personal brand as a service provider. Your personal brand should be a true representation of who you are and what you stand for. Consistency is key, as it helps to establish trust and credibility with your audience.

In conclusion, building your personal brand as a service provider can be a powerful tool for attracting new clients and growing your business. By defining your unique value proposition, developing your brand identity, creating your personal brand story, establishing yourself as an expert, leveraging testimonials and referrals, networking and collaborating, and being authentic and consistent, you can build a personal brand that sets you apart from your competitors and attracts the right clients.

Chapter 39

Building Your Personal Brand as a Job Seeker

In today's competitive job market, creating a personal brand has become increasingly important for job seekers. A personal brand can help you stand out from other candidates and enhance your career prospects. It is not just about having a strong resume or impressive qualifications, but also about showcasing your unique skills and values that make you a perfect fit for the job.

Here are some tips on how to build your personal brand as a job seeker:

1. Identify Your Unique Selling Points

The first step in building your personal brand as a job seeker is to identify your unique selling points. Think about what sets you apart from other candidates and what skills and experiences make you a perfect fit for the job. Make a list of your strengths and accomplishments, and use these to build your personal brand.

2. Create a Personal Brand Statement

Once you have identified your unique selling points, create a personal brand statement. This is a brief statement that highlights your skills, experience, and values. Your personal brand statement should be tailored to the job you are applying for and should showcase why you are the best candidate for the position.

3. Develop a Professional Online Presence

Having a professional online presence is crucial in today's job market. Start by creating a LinkedIn profile that showcases your skills and experiences. Make sure your profile picture is professional and your profile is complete. You can also consider creating a personal website or blog that showcases your work and expertise.

4. Showcase Your Expertise

One of the best ways to build your personal brand as a job seeker is to showcase your expertise. This can be done by creating content related to your field of work, such as blog posts, articles, or videos. You can also participate in online forums or communities related to your industry and share your knowledge and expertise.

5. Network and Build Relationships

Networking is an important part of building your personal brand as a job seeker. Attend industry events, connect with professionals in your field, and engage in online communities. Building relationships with other professionals can help you learn about job opportunities and gain insights into the industry.

6. Be Consistent

Consistency is key when it comes to building your personal brand as a job seeker. Make sure your personal brand statement, online presence, and networking efforts all align with your career goals and values. Consistency will help you build a strong personal brand that employers will remember.

In conclusion, building a personal brand as a job seeker is crucial for enhancing your career prospects. By identifying your unique selling points, creating a personal brand statement, developing a professional online presence, showcasing your expertise, networking, and being consistent, you can build a personal brand that sets you apart from other candidates and helps you achieve your career goals.

Chapter 40

Conclusion

Congratulations! You've made it through all of the chapters in this guide to building your brand on social media. By now, you should have a solid understanding of the importance of branding, how to create a brand strategy, and how to build and grow your brand on social media. You've learned about various tactics and strategies, from content creation to influencer marketing, that can help you increase your reach and engage with your target audience.

However, building a successful brand on social media is an ongoing process. It requires time, effort, and a willingness to adapt and evolve as the social media landscape changes. In this final chapter, we'll discuss how you can continue to build your brand on social media and ensure its longevity.

1. Keep creating valuable content

As we discussed earlier in this guide, content is king. It's the foundation of your brand's online presence and the key to building relationships with your audience. To keep your audience engaged and attract new followers, you need to continue to create valuable content on a regular basis. Use the insights you've gained from monitoring your social media analytics to understand what type of content resonates most with your audience and create more of it.

2. Engage with your audience

Social media is a two-way conversation. Engaging with your audience is a critical component of building and maintaining your brand. Respond to comments and messages, ask for feedback, and participate in relevant conversations. Show your audience that you value their input and appreciate their support.

3. Stay up-to-date on the latest trends

The social media landscape is constantly changing. New platforms and features are introduced regularly, and user behavior evolves over time. To keep your brand relevant, you need to stay up-to-date on the latest trends and best practices. Follow social media blogs, attend conferences and webinars, and monitor your competitors to understand what's working in your industry.

4. Collaborate with other brands and influencers

Collaborating with other brands and influencers can help you reach new audiences and establish your brand as an authority in your industry. Look for opportunities to partner with other brands or influencers whose values align with yours. Develop mutually beneficial partnerships that can help you both reach your goals.

5. Measure your success

Finally, to ensure that your brand is growing and achieving its goals, you need to measure your success. Use social media analytics tools to track your progress, monitor engagement rates and follower growth, and adjust your strategy as needed. Don't be afraid to try new things and experiment with different tactics. Keep learning and evolving your strategy over time.

Building a successful brand on social media is not an easy task, but it's a worthwhile one. By following the tips and strategies outlined in this guide, you'll be well on your way to establishing a strong brand presence online. Remember to stay focused, stay engaged with your audience, and keep experimenting to find what works best for you. Good luck!

As we come to the end of this book, we hope that you have gained a deeper understanding of the importance of building a strong and effective brand on social media. Whether you're a public figure, entrepreneur, professional, or creative, a strong personal brand can help you achieve your goals, establish your authority, and connect with your audience.

We have explored a variety of strategies and tactics for building your brand on social media, including creating valuable content, engaging with your followers, building a community, managing your reputation, and more. While each of these strategies is important on its own, it's the combination of all of them that will help you achieve long-term success.

Remember that building a brand is not a one-time project, but a continuous process. It requires patience, dedication, and a willingness to learn and adapt. With the right mindset and the right tools, you can create a brand that truly resonates with your audience and helps you achieve your goals.

We wish you all the best in your brand-building journey. May you continue to grow and thrive on social media and beyond.